202 TIPS

Even the Best Business Travelers May Not Know

202 TIPS

Even the Best Business Travelers May Not Know

Christopher J. McGinnis

IRWIN Professional Publishing
Burr Ridge, Illinois
New York, New York

Senior sponsoring editor: Cynthia A. Zigmund
Project editor: Jane Lightell
Production manager: Laurie Kersch
Interior designer: Electronic Publishing Services
Cover designer: Tim Kaage
Chapter sketches: Richard Jenrette
Art manager: Kim Meriwether
Compositor: Electronic Publishing Services
Typeface: 11/14 Palatino
Printer: R. R. Donnelley & Sons Company

Library of Congress Cataloging-in-Publication Data

McGinnis, Christopher J.
  202 tips even the best business travelers may not know
  Christopher J. McGinnis.
    p.   cm.
  Includes index.
    ISBN 1-55623-966-1   MCI Edition: ISBN 0-7863-0339-5
    1. Business travel.   I. Title.
  G156.5.B86M38   1994
  910'.2'02—dc20

                                                94–2846
                                                CIP

Printed in the United States of America
 2 3 4 5 6 7 8 9 0 DO-C 1 0 9 8 7 6 5 4

TO KATHY

ACKNOWLEDGMENTS

Primary thanks are due Tom Eblen, deputy business editor at the *Atlanta Journal-Constitution* for heeding my pleas for a *business* travel column (in the newspaper's business section) featuring tips and information for the "other half" of the travel market that the leisure travel section was leaving out. The resulting weekly column has been instrumental to my growth as a writer, the success of my business, and I hope, helpful to Atlanta business travelers.

Just as important to my career as a business travel writer are my editors Karen Axelton, "the Marias," and Rieva Lesonsky at *Entrepreneur Magazine*. They helped thrust my work into a national light, which resulted in Cynthia Zigmund of Irwin Professional Publishing tracking me down to make this book a reality. Thanks to all of them.

For helping me cope with the myriad changes and paradoxes in this dynamic (some say glamorous) industry, and as personal sounding boards for my ideas and brainstorms, I thank Bonita Smith at Century Travel and Chris Smith at WorldTravel Partners. Access to travel industry computerized reservations systems and data banks through these extraordinary business travel agents has made this book (and my work overall) much less complicated.

Special gratitude to my business travelers' roundtable: a group of creative, insightful, and dedicated road warriors, whose Saturday morning meetings at the Swissôtel-Atlanta spawned many of the road-tested tips and advice found in the coming pages. Thanks Bill Creedon, Mark Abbonizio, Shirley Walker, Tom Flach, Doug Duke, Jeff Chauvin, Bryant Gresham, John Kirtland, Carol Baum, Ted Haslam, Bartow Rainey, Jim Bierma, William Mills III, and Albert Blesgraeft.

Happy travels!

Christopher J. McGinnis

CONTENTS

Chapter

1 Introduction 1

PART I **THE TRIP**

2 Things to Know before You Go 7

3 What to Bring, How to Bring It 19

4 Getting to and from the Airport 27

5 Surviving the Airport 37

6 On the Plane 51

7 On the Road: Renting/Driving Cars 63

8 At the Hotel 71

9 Using the Telephone 83

PART II **GENERAL INFORMATION**

10 Frequent Traveler Programs 91

11 International Travel 101

12 Eating Right 119

13 Staying Healthy and Managing Stress 129

APPENDIX Business Travel Telephone Resources 139

Introduction

In 1984 I took my first business trip. I had just completed the Master's program at the American Graduate School of International Management ("Thunderbird") in Phoenix, Arizona. Sea-Land, the containerized shipping company, invited me to New York for a job interview.

I remember the "important" feeling I had when booking my airline ticket through their company travel agency. The agent reserved a room for me at the Holiday Inn "Jetport" at Newark airport. The company even thought enough of me to express mail the tickets to Arizona the following day. Wow! This was the big time! Bright-eyed and eager, I must have read over my itinerary, tickets, and boarding passes at least a dozen times.

When the big day arrived, I packed a suit in my hang up bag, the resume in my briefcase, and headed off to the airport. This time I wasn't going home for the holidays or off on Spring break. This was a business trip! A bit apprehensive of this new role, I watched the briefcase and trenchcoat crowd for cues—look straight ahead, walk fast, keep a pen in your pocket, feign indifference, don't check your bag, do some work on the plane, and generally, act serious.

I arrived at my hotel in Newark at dusk. In my room overlooking the runways, I watched planes take off into the sunset, ate a room service club sandwich, pondered life, and worried about my interview. Little did I know that this transcontinental trip and Holiday Inn stay would be much more meaningful to my true calling than the impending interview.

Not that I didn't get the job with Sea-Land. I did, and it is with them I took my first few steps as a business traveler. However, the real frequent traveling began when I accepted my second job as a trainer with a management consulting company. This job demanded travel every Sunday night through Friday night.

For the next three years, I lived on airplanes and at airports, stayed at hundreds of hotels, drove thousands of miles in rental cars, made countless long-distance credit-card calls, missed my family and friends, and got hooked on the then-nascent frequent traveler programs. I soon found that I was much more enamored of the travel industry than the consulting business. Naturally, I became my company's resident travel guru.

This company had a reputation for inducting young Turks from business schools, chewing them up for a couple years, then spitting them out. Exit interviews showed that most of those who quit left because of "the travel." Having doled out mountains of advice to the semi-annual class of new recruits, or "green peas,"I suggested to management that part of our company's training program be devoted to teaching the "art" of frequent travel—a "traveler training" program. Official response: lukewarm at best.

But I knew I had an idea that would work. Business travel had evolved into a complex, intimidating, and often mis-understood part of modern corporate life. A 1994 MCI/Gallup survey of 500 business travelers determined that only 19 percent felt that business travel was "fun" or "glamorous," while 89 percent thought that non-travelers felt that frequent travel was fun or glamorous. Fifty-three percent of the group said that being away from loved ones and missing day-to-day events was a problem.

Business travelers no longer flew from City A to City B, did their job, then came home. With airline deregulation, the frequent traveler marketplace had exploded: everything became negotiable, telephones and long distance calling were different, airline travel had become a maze of new fares, rules, and restrictions, hotels offered unheard of choices like concierge levels and video check-out, credit cards changed, and car rental contracts became fine-print gobbledygook.

To me, it was obvious. Business travelers everywhere needed help. For many companies and individuals, learning how to travel on-the-job was the hard and expensive way. At just about that time, the Marriott Business Travel Institute published the results of a survey that concluded that although companies were spending almost $100 billion a year on travel and entertainment, only 5 percent of business travelers had ever received any formal training on how to make travel better. But 87 percent of the travelers and

93 percent of travel managers surveyed thought that training would definitely yield benefits.

Reading that survey in *USA TODAY* on a flight to Bozeman, Montana, pushed me over the edge. I would do it on my own. So I quit the consulting company and launched Travel Skills Group in 1988. Since then we have trained thousands of frequent travelers at companies across the country. Our columns, newsletters, and interviews in the national media have helped countless others to learn "the art of traveling smart."

This book is a compendium of much of what we have learned and taught over the last six years. In the coming pages, you will find a "one room schoolhouse approach," meaning that the 202 tips that follow should apply to both novice and seasoned travelers.

Everyone will find at least a few "a-ha's" or "I-never-knew-that's" in the coming pages. Anyone who is currently, or plans to travel in this "new world order" of business travel will benefit from our tips and advice. Even business travel industry professionals will benefit from the book by passing the information on to their frequent traveling clients.

We present our information as a series of quickly read, easily grasped, and retained tips—helpful, useful, or interesting nuggets of information to make your life on the road better. Some tips are one liners. Others are headings for a series of tips on a general subject. At the end of some chapters, you'll find something for nothing: a series of un-numbered "bonus" tips that will help make your travels safer and more secure.

Part One of the book is set up chronologically, from trip planning, packing, and getting to the airport, through the flight, drive, and hotel stay. Part Two provides general tips that you can (and should!) use at any point in your travels, from foreign currency exchange to eating alone, or staying fit on the road.

So, begin your journey right now by picking up a few tips on . . .

CHAPTER 2

Tips 1–19
Things to Know before You Go

| 1 | **Stay Inside the Information Loop** |

Read up! Stay in tune with the travel industry. Aside from what you are holding in your hands, here are some of the best sources of business travel information:

- *USA TODAY*'s Money section. In addition to the industry news reported in this section, a special column (aptly called "Business Travel") appears every Tuesday. Also watch for its excellent business travel pullout sections (every April, June, September) compiled by a staff of reporters devoted to this subject alone.

- *The Wall Street Journal*'s "Tracking Travel" column. Appearing periodically on the front of the Marketplace (B) section is an excellent, topical, source of travel industry news.

- The Sunday *New York Times* Travel section. Although mostly devoted to leisure travel, you'll find periodic reporting on business travel topics. Especially helpful is a regular feature (usually on page 3 or 4) called "The Practical Traveler." Your local paper's Sunday Travel section should also be a source of business travel information, but most are pretty weak in this area. However, some smart local papers now carry local or syndicated columns addressing the business traveler in their business sections.

- Travel magazines. *Travel and Leisure* adds a few extra pages to the magazines mailed to subscribers whose American Express cards indicate heavy airline usage. (Called "Business Trip".)

Condé Nast *Traveler* also includes good business travel tips in its introductory pages.

- Business travel magazines and newsletters. There's a plethora, but the best include: *InsideFlyer* for frequent traveler program information ($33/yr., or free trial issue, tel.: 800-333-5937), *Frequent Flyer* (usually sent with the *Official Airline Guide*) provides good national/international coverage ($24/yr., tel.: 800-323-3537), *Best Fares*, which helps travelers with back-to-back or hidden city fares and other travel deals ($58/yr., tel.: 800-635-3033). Hard-core information seekers should look into trade publications *Business Travel News* or *Corporate Travel* (tel.: 800-964-9494).

- Other sources: Frequent flyer program statements, travel agency newsletters, and the best source—other business travelers.

| 2 | **Choose a Good Travel Agent** |

Do you think travel agents lead a glamorous life consisting of some work, but mostly play? Do you think they probably spend more time on warm beaches than at their desks? Think again. High pressure, high turnover, thin profit margins, cutthroat competition, complex technology, and a constantly changing product are the realities of the travel agency business. In almost all cases, it is wiser to use a trusted travel agent than to call travel suppliers directly. But how do you find a good travel agent?

- First define the services you need from a travel agent—write them down.

- Ask around. Finding a good travel agent is like finding a good doctor. Use your network of business contacts, friends, or consultants for recommendations. When you find a good one, stick with him or her.

- Meet the agency owners and managers. Be sure you are comfortable with them. Let them know that you are seeking a long-term relationship. Meet the agents. How long have they been in the business? How familiar are they with your specific travel needs?

- Find out if the agency is biased toward certain air carriers. Some travel agencies earn overrides or percentage points that are added to the standard 10 percent commission the airlines pay only if they favor one airline (and can prove it). If that is the case, you may not always get the lowest fare. However, agencies with these relationships are in a better position to "pull strings" with favored airlines to get their clients out of travel jams.

- Does the agency utilize a computerized "low fare finder" or "seat finder?" These programs constantly scan the reservations systems for better deals or better seats after you've made your reservation, and rebook you if they find them.

- Some agencies are better at leisure travel than business travel, although few will admit it. (You may not want to use a business travel agent to book your honeymoon on Nevis nor a leisure travel agent to book your four-city sales junket.)

AIRLINE RESERVATIONS

Airfares are confusing to even the most seasoned traveler. Some clarification:

| 3 | The lowest fare available (discounted coach) is usually not used by business travelers because it requires a Saturday night stayover, charges penalties for changes, and is nonrefundable. |

| 4 | Most of the upstart low-fare, or niche carriers now offer low unrestricted fares between a growing number of cities. Most do not require a Saturday night stayover. |

| 5 | More expensive full-coach fares are the best option for midweek flying travelers. No Saturday night stay is required. There are no penalties for changes or refunds. |

| 6 | Minimally restricted business-class fares are only available on transcontinental or international flights. |

| 7 | First-class fares carry the same minimal restrictions as full-coach fares. Members of airline frequent travel programs can sometimes ask for special discounts on first-class fares. |

| 8 | To save money, many business travelers are turning to more restricted discounted coach fares that require a Saturday night stay. Rules for these tickets are confusing and vary considerably between airlines, but generally: |

- Nonrefundable fares have a maximum stay of 30 days.

- The return flight can be changed for an airline-imposed fee (currently $25–$50) provided a discount seat is available.

- The outbound flight can only be changed if the same fare is still offered and the advance purchase requirement is met. Again, the service fee will apply.

- If the same fare is not offered, ask for the best available nonrefundable fare and apply your original ticket toward it. You will then pay any fare difference including the service fee.

- Partially used, nonrefundable tickets generally have no refund value and cannot be applied toward another ticket.

---

9 | Get Creative with Ticketing

Business travelers typically fly midweek and cannot take advantage of cheaper airfares that require a Saturday night stayover. This unfortunately forces the cost conscious to "bend the rules" to find affordable fares. To save money, consider using these creative ticketing strategies:

- A "back-to-back" fare works when (for a midweek trip) it is cheaper to buy two round-trip tickets that require a Saturday night stay than one unrestricted, full-coach fare. "Back-to-backers" simply use the outbound portion of each ticket. Savings can be as much as 50 percent.

- A "hidden city" fare is created when competing air carriers are forced to meet fare pricing set by a competitor within a certain market. In doing so, carriers will sometimes offer a lower fare to a destination that connects through one of their higher priced hub cities. To take advantage of hidden city fares, book your flight to the least expensive city (beyond your final destination) and simply get off when the plane stops at the higher priced hub city. Warning: Carry on all luggage to avoid it being sent to the ticketed destination. (Previously referenced *Best Fares* can help you with these fares.)

---

10 | Make Proper Hotel, Car Rental Reservations

- Always write down your hotel and car rental confirmation numbers on your airline ticket jacket or in your daily organizer. These numbers are vital if your reservation is lost, the computers are down, or if you are denied your room or car.

- When getting your confirmation number, ask for your reservationist's name. Psychologically, the reservationist will most likely be sure that all parts of your reservation are correct if he/she knows his/her name is attached to it.

- A hotel room is *reserved* until 6 PM. A hotel room is *guaranteed* until whenever you get there—even if you don't. Know the difference.

- Most car rental companies have more large cars than small ones. By reserving a compact car at a cheap rate, the chances are that when you arrive and a compact is not available, you'll be upgraded to a larger car, free of charge. If you in fact get the compact, the agent will most likely ask if you would like to upgrade for a fee that is usually less than if you reserved a larger car.

- If you will be late to pick up your car, call the car rental company if possible. They will typically hold the car you have requested for only an hour after your scheduled arrival. If you don't make your scheduled arrival time, you may be forced to pay for a larger car, or find no car at all.

- To get the lowest rate, you must ask for it two or three times throughout the reservation process. Reservationists are trained to not give away the store if they don't have to. *Ask:* Is this the lowest rate available? Are there any specials on now? Can I get a better deal? Is the corporate rate the lowest rate? What other cheaper rates are available? What would I have to do to qualify for the cheapest rate?

| 11 | Use Airline On-Time Performance Data

Most surveys indicate that business travelers' top concern about air travel is on-time performance. The Department of Transportation tracks the airlines in this regard and publishes statistics in their monthly Consumer Report.

- Always ask for the on-time performance of the flight you are reserving. Your travel agent or reservationist has a number on their screen ranking the flight on a scale of 1–10. A 1 indicates the flight was on time at least 10 percent of the time in the previous month; 9 means the flight was on time at least 90 percent of the time in the previous month.

- Avoid flights that depart or land during airport rush hours that typically run between 9–11 AM or 4–8 PM.

| 12 | **Beware of Travel Scams** |

Beware: "Travel scams" involving so-called free or bargain, or other assorted too-good-to-be-true trips (business or vacation) that are in reality rip-offs are on the rise, according to the American Society of Travel Agents. Warning signs of potentially bogus offers:

- An unsolicited call and an unwillingness to provide the complete company name, street address, and phone number.

- Pressure to make a quick decision and provide your credit card number on the spot, or a request for payment before receiving full information about the trip.

- A price that seems unbelievably low.

- Refusal to name the hotels where you will stay or the airlines or cruise line on which you will travel. (Be wary of vague replies like "major" hotels or "major" airlines.)

- A requirement to wait at least 60 days to get confirmed reservations or to take the trip after making payment. This is usually an attempt to use up the 60-day time limit that a credit card customer has to challenge the charge with the bank.

MORE PRETRIP TIPS:

| 13 | Reserve your special airline meal at least 24 hours in advance, and reconfirm your request when you check in. |

| 14 | Watch out for huge trade shows or sporting events that can clog a city's airport and fill hotels unexpectedly. |

| 15 | If there is more than one Marriott or Hyatt in the city where you are going, be sure you know which one you are in. |

| 16 | Write all your frequent traveler program numbers and frequently called 800 numbers on a pocket-sized piece of paper for easy access. |

| 17 | Always request a seat assignment and ask that your boarding pass be sent with your airline tickets when making reservations. |

| 18 | Sometimes calling a hotel directly, bypassing your travel agent or the hotel's 800 reservations line, can net savings. Ask for the best deal available that day. Also, there are now companies that buy hotels rooms in bulk at discount prices, then pass the savings on to travelers booking through them (i.e., The Hotel Reservations Network, 1-800-96-HOTELS). |

19 A nonstop flight means just that—no stops. A direct flight means that the plane will stop at least once before reaching your final destination. Know the difference.

Tips 20–36
What to Bring, How to Bring It

PACKING

Frequent travel is as tough on bags as it is on travelers. Proper packing and lugging can help make a business trip easy. Pack too much and you'll strain your body, wrinkle your clothes, and run into delays with skycaps and porters or at baggage claim. Choose the wrong type of luggage and watch it turn into a ball and chain. Read on for tips that help keep you light on your feet and looking good.

| 20 | Choosing the Best Luggage |

- Don't sacrifice strength and durability for price. Look for bags with heavy-duty stitching and zippers, metal buckles, and padded handles or shoulder straps. If you can afford leather, buy it. Otherwise, look for heavy-duty "ballistic" nylon, or nylon and leather combinations. Color? When in doubt, opt for black—it doesn't show scuffs and always looks good.

- How about a good set of "wheels?" Although eschewed by many frequent travelers, luggage trollies are used almost universally by flight attendants—the ultimate road warriors. But, more and more business travelers are trying them these days. When buying wheels, again, opt for durability over price. The cheapest chrome-plated versions may wear out after only a trip or two through a major airport.

- For those who think of wheels as too unwieldy, consider "roll-aboard" type suitcases. These carry-on-sized suitcases are typically made of durable black nylon with built-in wheels and an extension handle that adjusts to the traveler's height. Increasingly popular "roll-aboard" type bags are the choice among flight attendants.

- If you have a common brand of luggage, tie a piece of unique yarn or ribbon on the handle to make quick identification easy.

- Remember, personal luggage tags are easily shorn from bags. Be sure that you have proper identification inside as well as outside your bag; remove all old airline-issued claim tags.

---

21 | Choosing the Best Clothing

- Key word: black. It is classic and works well in almost every situation. Just don't forget your lint brush.

- Bring clothes that you can mix and match. If embarking on a longer two- or three-suit trip, try to bring all outfits with the same general color scheme. Blacks, grays, khakis work well. Don't bring anything that you can't mix and match.

- Although expensive, hotel valet and laundry services are well worth not having to haul around more clothes than you need.

---

22 | Avoiding Wrinkles

- Wool or cotton and polyester blends do not wrinkle as much as pure wool or 100 percent cotton. Don't even think about traveling with linen.

- Pack clothes in the plastic bags from the dry cleaners.

- Hang wrinkled clothes in the bathroom and close the door during your shower. Wrinkles will fall out.

- Most hotels will supply an iron and ironing board on request.

- If not carrying a hang-up bag, men should ask cleaners to fold rather than hang their shirts for better packing.

---

23 Two axioms to remember: "If you have to check it, don't bring it," and "Bring half as many clothes and twice as much money."

---

24 Pack larger items first, then stuff rolled-up underwear, socks, or other items around them.

---

25 Toilet kit suggestions:

- If you are a regular traveler, have a toilet kit permanently packed with your usual items for use on the road only. This keeps you from having to reassemble your kit each time you take a trip.

- Buy a set of plastic travel-sized bottles (available at many drugstores) for packing your potions and lotions. Don't fill them to the top as changes in aircraft cabin pressure cause leaks. Pack all liquids together in a zip-lock bag. Be sure aerosols (shave cream, mousse, hairspray) have their plastic protective tops attached.

| 26 | Pack shoes in plastic bags to avoid soiling your clothes. |

| 27 | Keep a roll of Scotch tape in your bag all the times. It can be used to quickly mend hems, seal bottles, or remove lint (from those black outfits). |

| 28 | Don't fret about whether or not you have packed everything you could conceivably need. Remember that you can buy just about anything you may need at your destination. |

| 29 | Consider "excess valuation insurance" at about $1 per $100 in declared value if you are checking expensive or valuable items. |

| 30 | Remove or secure the hang-up hook from your hang-up bag when in transit. Loose hooks easily snag on airport luggage-moving systems. |

LUGGING

| 31 | If you are carrying on a big bag, get on the plane as early as possible. Overhead bins fill up fast— particularly during the cold winter months and during the holidays. |

| 32 | Once on the plane, don't place your bag in an overhead bin behind you. (Meaning that when the plane unloads, you'll have to go upstream to retrieve it.) Get it in the bin ahead of you, if possible. |

| 33 | If you bring more than two carry-ons (the official limit) and the gate agent is being strict, you can always ask a less burdened and friendly looking person near you in line to carry on one bag—or put a bag inside a bag. Gate agents usually scrutinize the number of bags more often than bag dimensions (FAA regulations: one no larger than 9" x 14" x 22" (can fit under seat) and another 10" x 14" x 36" (can fit in overhead bin) or a 4" x 23" x 45" garment bag (can fit in closet). Note: a briefcase is considered a piece of carry-on luggage, whereas a woman's purse may not be.

| 34 | You can always have your bag "gate checked" if you are running late and can't check it at the counter. The best part about gate-checked bags is that they are usually waiting by the plane door as you exit—not at the delay prone baggage carousel.

| 35 | If traveling by car, pack a smaller bag for hotel/motel stops en route. This way you don't have to lug your heavy bags into every hotel or motel on the way. Important: be sure that the bags you do leave in your car are out of sight. Use your judgment in deciding whether it is smart to leave anything in the car overnight.

| 36 | Tired of hauling your bags back and forth between your home and the same hotel every week? Inquire about leaving your bags at the hotel. Also, many "business" hotels are empty on weekends. Inquire about the possibility of simply leaving your clothes in your room without charge. |

Tips 37–54
Getting to and from the Airport

Every journey begins with a single step, so the saying goes. Well, almost every business trip begins and ends with a single trip to and from the airport. And the trip between the airport and your meeting or your home could be more involved and arduous than a 2,000-mile journey across the country.

Has this ever happened to you?

Your 5 PM flight has landed and you've retrieved your bags. Now you want to get into town and your hotel is only guaranteed until 6 PM. What's the best way? How much will a cab cost? Is there an airport limo or van? How often? How long does it take? Is there a rapid rail link that could beat traffic?

Or... your meeting has just ended and your flight home leaves in an hour. You are in a strange city and you have to pick the fastest way to get to the airport. What do you do? Airport transit choices are many and sometimes confusing. Speed, comfort, and cost are all factors in your choice. The key is to find the way that optimally combines all three. More tips:

---

37 Do not take the first conveyance you see as you exit the terminal—usually a taxicab—unless you know that is exactly what you need. Other factors to consider: Are you on a tight budget? Do you have too much luggage for the subway? Are you in a party of two or more? Do you need to recover your mental resources in the comfort of a limousine before a big meeting? Are you in the city for the first time?

| 38 | Travel agents can usually tell you in advance the various means of transportation available from the airport that you are flying into to the nearby city or outlying communities. |

| 39 | In larger cities, the airport authority usually operates a local or ground transportation desk near the baggage claim area to assist travelers in making frugal, intelligent, and safe choices. Don't accept rides from anyone who approaches you in the terminal unless you have already made prior arrangements. |

YOUR OPTIONS

| 40 | **By Taxi** |

- In most major cities you can just walk out of the airport or into the street and hail one. In smaller towns, beware—or plan ahead. There may not be enough taxis, and getting one could mean a long wait.

- Most taxis have a laundry list of extra fees that you need to be wary of. Surcharges for ordering a cab by phone, per piece of luggage, airport pick-up, time-of-day, and additional passengers seem to be at the driver's discretion. It is best to first ask how much your ride will cost—before the trip begins—even if there is a meter.

- Better yet, ask a friend or a hotel concierge for a ballpark figure for how much you should spend on a cab to the airport. If you feel gypped, ask for a receipt with the driver's name and meter number on it.

---

41 | By Car Services

⊚ Most prevalent in New York, but spreading to other cities. Sometimes limo companies offer car services—a "right-sized" version of their usual offering. Car services represent a good value because they set a flat fee. Unexpected traffic delays can sometimes hike cab fares, which are usually based on an equation of distance traveled and time.

• In 1993 car services (listed below) in New York City charged a flat $15.00 plus a $2.50 toll to go to and from La Guardia Airport and $25.00 plus a $2.50 toll to or from Newark or Kennedy Airports. (Remember, we are talking about New York City here, so don't forget to tip the driver.)

To book a car service, call from home before you leave. Three good New York City car services are:

Tel Aviv at (212) 777-7777.
Jerusalem at (212) 996-6600.
Sabra at (212) 777-7171.

---

42 | By Rail/Subway/Train

• Rail connections are by far the most economical and fastest way to go—especially during rush hours. Rapid rail service is inside or a very close walk or shuttle ride from airports in Atlanta, Boston, Cleveland, Chicago, Oakland, Philadelphia, and Washington, DC.

Rapid rail costs:

Atlanta	$1.25
Boston	$ .85
Chicago	$1.50
Cleveland	$1.25
Philadelphia	$4.50
Washington	$1.00–$1.25
Oakland	$2.00

43 | By Bus/Van

- Privately operated shuttle bus services, like the Carey Airport Express, Olympia Trails, or Gray Line bus services from the New York City airports offer an excellent alternative to high-priced cabs. Also, the blue "Airporter" (or similar) vans operating in many major cities bring passengers wherever they want to go in a specific area—for a fraction of what a cab would cost.

- Going from airport to city by municipally operated bus is really not a viable option for most business travelers. However, if you are a hardcore penny pincher, inquire at the airport ground transportation counter.

44 | Family Members

- Always have a designated pick-up area at the airport in case all else fails. Having a regular back up meeting spot helps avoid the problems associated with flight delays, traffic delays, and miscommunication.

45 | Hotel Shuttle

- Many business travelers forget to ask about this (usually) free service when making their reservations and end up paying exorbitant cab fares when they could have gone for free. Actually, courtesy airport shuttle services are built into your hotel rate, so if you don't use them you are actually paying twice.

A HELPFUL RESOURCE

Many travel agents, corporate travel managers, and travelers rely on the Salk International Airport Transit Guide, a complete guide on airport transfers to more than 400 airports around the world. The pocket-sized guide, revised each October, provides taxi rates and tipping guidelines to each city, airport coach, limo, and van fares and schedules, public transit fares, schedules and routes, airport parking rates, car rental facilities, and helicopter services. Typically, travel agents, airlines, or hotels give the guide to their clients as premiums, but they can be ordered directly from: Salk International, PO Box 1388, Sunset Beach, CA, 90742, CA, tel.: (714) 893-0812. Some pearls of wisdom from the guide (based on early 1994 prices):

46 | At Milan's Linate Airport, legal taxis are yellow or white with blue stripes. All others are gypsy cabs, where the normal $18 ride might wind up costing you twice as much.

47 | At Tokyo's Narita Airport, now called New Tokyo International, a 60- to 90-minute cab ride

will cost over $190! (Instead, take the $15, 25-minute train.)

---

48 In many cities around the world, travelers will usually find a bank of courtesy phones near the baggage claim area at the airport. It is wise to check there first to see if your hotel provides free shuttle service.

---

49 A broad array of conveyances are available to get you to the city from most large airports. In Boston, try the Airport Water Shuttle. A free van leaves every 5–10 minutes from the airport to the water shuttle that takes passengers to Rowe's Wharf, next to the Boston Harbor Hotel. The boat leaves every 15 minutes, costs $8, and takes 7 minutes to cross the harbor. Delta offers water shuttle service from New York's La Guardia Airport to Manhattan.

---

50 At Chicago-O'Hare, a moving sidewalk transports you to the entrance of the CTA subway/elevated train station where for only $1.50 you are transported to the Loop in under 40 minutes. Some cars have baggage space. (Not advised during rush hours, but otherwise an economical and efficient transfer, says Salk.)

---

51 From Munich's new airport (opened in May 1992), the S-Bahn train #8 travels the 17.5 miles into this bustling Bavarian city in 41 minutes for about $7.50.

52 In Paris, the Air France coach system is continually improving and provides excellent service to many points, and even offers special prices for three or four people. And Paris is continually adding new transfer services by bus, train, and limousine.

53 In Geneva, the ultramodern rail link between Cointrin Airport and the main rail station is the best service business travelers could ask for. Departures are every 10 minutes, the fare is about $3, and there is plenty of baggage space. And talking about Switzerland, Swissrail and Swissair jointly offer a superb check-in service at rail stations all over the country. You can check-in your bags and get your boarding pass for your flight at the train station. Conversely, you can have your luggage checked through Swissair at the beginning of your trip to your final destination in Switzerland by rail. There is a $12 charge for the service, but it is well worth it and very reliable.

54 In Frankfurt, Lufthansa has a masterful system of buses and trains that speed business travelers to many points throughout the country. The train segments carry flight numbers and are prebooked with your airline ticket.

The Lufthansa Deluxe Intercity train operates four times daily along the scenic Rhine River between Frankfurt and Dusseldorf airports with intermediate stops in Bonn, Cologne, and Dusseldorf Central Station. The train also operates from Stuttgart four times per day. These supertrains are booked with flight numbers on your air ticket. Lufthansa passengers pay nothing extra for the rail segments and have the option of taking the faster, more convenient train or a Lufthansa flight segment. Business travel veterans most always recommend the train. It is first-class—with food, drink, and "flight attendants." Air traffic congestion combined with faster, more efficient trains may soon render intra-German air travel obsolete.

CHAPTER 5

Tips 55–80
Surviving the Airport

Most business travelers know something about their rights at the airport. But most of what you may know is through hearsay, or the occasional war story heard from a fellow traveler stuck in a scary situation. This chapter will provide you with the facts about your rights as travelers, and how to assert those rights when the need arises. We also provide some other general and safety tips that should help you survive any airport.

TRAVELERS' RIGHTS

Since deregulation, government protection for air travelers is limited to three areas: limits of liability for lost and damaged luggage, rules for overbooking and bumping, and enforcement of the smoking ban on domestic flights.

---

55 By law, the airlines must provide travelers with a copy of their "Contract of Carriage" on request. If you are interested, contact the airlines' legal division and they will mail you one. Although a rare find, the contract should also (by law) be on hand at city ticket offices.

---

56 The best way to look out for your rights? First, know what they are (by reading this chapter, of course, or reading a contract of carriage). Second, ask if you feel your rights are being violated. This is a major point . . . *always ask!* With deregulation the airlines are no longer required to offer any compensation for inconvenience. But, they are customer-oriented businesses, and they will try to help . . . but usually only on request.

Flight Delays

| 57 | Your first step in a delay should be to head to the nearest pay phone and find out why the flight is delayed. Call the other airlines (don't waste a quarter, use their 800 numbers); see if their flights are experiencing similar delays. Look around at other gates. Are their flights leaving on time? |

| 58 | If you suspect that you are being delayed for something other than a weather or air traffic problem, approach the gate agent and confidently assert your suspicion, give a reason why you cannot wait, and ask to be booked on the next flight out on that airline, or a competing airline. This is called Rule 240 and all the major airlines include it in their contract of carriage. What Rule 240 does is tell the original carrier to pick up the tab for any additional expense in getting you to your intended destination via another carrier. Rule 240 applies to other direct flights to your final destination as well as any connecting flights that may exist. When you really want or need to get out of town, ask the gate agent: "Can you 240 me?" (It is important to use their lingo.) They will code your ticket, and you will be on your way. |

| 59 | Refer to your OAG (*Official Airline Guide*) or other comprehensive schedule of all airlines to and from all destinations. These come in handy when you are trying to make a quick getaway from the mass confusion and hysteria that surround delay |

or cancellation announcements. (OAG, $86/yr. 1-800-323-3537.)

FLIGHT CANCELLATIONS

| 60 | As in delay situations, go to an airport pay phone as soon as you hear a call for cancellation, and make a reservation on the next flight to your destination on that airline or a competing airline. Most of the time airline personnel will try to book everyone on *their* next flight out. Shrewd travelers know that the gate agents will put you on a *competitor*'s next flight only if you ask.

OTHER SECRETS

| 61 | Of course, the simplest way to avoid delay and cancellation situations is to fly airlines that maintain good on-time performance rankings, or fly at times that the skies are not so congested. (Your chances of being delayed are greatest from 4 PM until 9 PM.)

| 62 | You can actually ask for the on-time performance of any flight when you make your reservation. Most travelers don't know about this, but the on-time performance for individual flights is tracked monthly on all reservations systems. When making your reservations, ask the agent for the on-time performance of the flight, and you will be given a score for the flight on a scale of 1–9 with 1 meaning that the flight was on time between 1 percent and 10 percent of the time, and 9 meaning

that the flight was on time 90 percent to 100 percent of the time in the preceding month. The airlines do not openly publicize this, so few people ever inquire. Always ask if being on time is crucial in your decision.

GETTING BUMPED

---

63 To get your requested seat and avoid being bumped, you must obey the ticketing and check-in requirements spelled out in the contract of carriage of each airline to exercise your rights. These requirements vary from airline to airline. You can sometimes find them listed on the ticket jacket. For most airlines, this means getting to the gate or your seat at least 10 to 20 minutes before departure if you already have your boarding pass. You should get there at least 30 minutes before departure if all you have is a phoned-in reservation. The 10- to 20-minute requirements are strict, and you must obey them if you want to assert your rights when you are bumped. (You are basically breaking your agreement with the airline if you can't meet them. In that case, they can give your seat to someone else, and you'll get no compensation.)

---

64 The DOT requires airlines to ask for volunteers before denying booked passengers waiting for seats. Volunteers are entitled to whatever the airline offers them; usually a free round-trip. However, many airlines offer only space available or standby free tickets as their first ante. These are difficult to use and cost the airline nothing to offer, so before you volunteer, make sure you are getting a confirmed round-trip ticket. Also be sure that the airline is going to book you on the next available flight out.

65 Better for frequent traveler program members is a travel voucher or a certificate of specific monetary value to apply to future flights on that airline. The voucher should always be worth at least the face value of the ticket you are holding. Travel vouchers are better for frequent travelers because you can still earn frequent flyer mileage on tickets "bought" in exchange for them. Travel on "free" bump coupons does not accrue frequent flyer miles.

66 When ticket agents have to sweeten the pot to get volunteers, they are empowered to give cash, travel vouchers, and meal vouchers. Sometimes you can ask for free long-distance phone calls, or get a pass to the airline's airport club to wait for your next flight.

67 Another good time to consult your OAG is when agents begin to ask for volunteers. If you find several flights to your destination departing immediately following yours, volunteer, get your free ticket or other compensation, then get booked on the next flight out.

68 If you ever get involuntarily bumped (meaning you have met the 10–20-minute cutoff and the airline still denies you a seat): You can ask to be rebooked, or 240ed on another airline. But if this flight gets you to your destination between one and two hours late, you are entitled to an amount equal to the price of your one-way fare, up to a maximum of $200. If you are more than two hours late, you are entitled to twice the value of your one-way ticket, up to a maximum of $400. Many times you can also keep your original ticket for a refund or future use. Remember: Bumping is more common during the holidays or busy summer months.

LOST BAGS

| 69 | One little-known fact is that airlines will reimburse you for out-of-pocket expenses associated with baggage delays. This usually includes toilet articles and some articles of clothing or some petty cash to buy them. You must ask for these things.

| 70 | DOT regulations state that if the airline loses your bag, they are only required to reimburse you for a maximum of $1,250 for the depreciated value of the declared contents. Standard operating procedure is for the airlines to automatically depreciate your claim by 30 percent. International travelers are reimbursed for lost baggage based on the weight of their bags (under the Warsaw Convention). Currently $9.07 per pound is all you'll get if your bags are lost on an international flight. So, if your bags are lost and you are asked

to estimate the value of the contents of your bags, err on the high side.

71 To minimize really big losses, buy *excess valuation* insurance when you check your bag. This insurance typically costs about $1 per $100 in value that you declare—in excess of the $1,250 automatic coverage.

COMPLAINING

72 Address complaints to US Department of Transportation, Consumer Affairs Division, Room 10405, 400 7th St. SW, Washington, DC, 20590. Or call: 202-366-2220.

73 Complain to (or compliment) the airlines. Telephone numbers of the major airlines' consumer affairs offices:

Alaska (206) 431 7286
American (817) 967 2000
America West (602) 693 6019
Continental (713) 987 6500
Delta (404) 715 1450
Northwest (612) 726 2046
Southwest (214) 904 4223
TWA (914) 242 3172
United (708) 952 6796
US Air (703) 892 7020

GENERAL AIRPORT TIPS

74 Join an airline airport club, a true refuge from the mob scene that sometimes forms at airports.

These are also excellent places to avoid having to wait in line for seat assignment changes or other ticketing problems. Many provide complimentary cocktails, beverages, and snacks. (Delta's Crown Room is the only one to offer free cocktails universally.) Beware though, hub and spoke systems have caused many clubs to be overcrowded—especially during airport rush hours.

75 If you are flying nonstop to or between smaller, non-hub airports, you can check your bags without too much fear of loss or delay.

76 Always have your travel agent or reservationist provide you with your boarding pass before you get to the airport. Remember, if you have a boarding pass, you do not have to check in at all—just hand your pass to the gate agent and walk on. A boarding pass helps in bump situations too.

77 The airport waitlist for upgrades or standby seats is not compiled on a first come, first served basis. It is based on a formula of frequent flier program status, the fare you paid, and whether or not you are in an emergency situation.

78 Ticketing and gate agents have been given great authority over enforcing airline rules, so it pays to be nice to them. Be calm and ask for their help— never demand it. When you slam your briefcase down on the counter, flash your frequent flyer card, and start to yell, they are more likely to play by the book.

---

79 | "Charm" your way into first class.

- Be nice, charming, inquisitive, never demanding.

- Good lines: "I had a dream I flew first class," "I threw my back/leg/shoulder out and need some room to stretch out," "We're on our honeymoon (buff those rings!)," "I just flew in from Bangkok."

- Use subtle bribery. Give the gate agent a rose from one of the airport concourse vendors.

---

80 | PLAY IT SAFE! Bonus Tips

- BEWARE OF DANGERS IN THE PARKING LOT
  Major city airports have muffled an increasing number of airport parking lot crimes. Try to park in well-lighted and close-in spaces—even if it costs more. Another safer option would be to use the new privately operated "off-airport" lots that have sprung up recently. These lots are usually well tended and offer regular shuttle service to the main terminal.

- LABEL BAGS INSIDE AND OUTSIDE
  Outside tags have a tendency to be shorn from bags in airport luggage handling systems. Best to label your bag inside and out. Some business travelers prefer to list their business address only. Listing a home address could lead to a burglary if the scoundrel that took your bag wants to hit your house too.

- CHECK LUGGAGE TAGS AFTER THE AGENT TIES THEM ON

Gate agents make mistakes, so be vigilant in double checking that your bags have the correct label affixed to them. Those three-letter airport codes can be confusing. Some three-letter codes make perfect sense—Atlanta, for example is ATL, but many don't—especially smaller airports. Knoxville, Tennessee's "TYS" code makes sense only if you know that the airport is named McGhee Tyson.

Some big city airports with confusing codes include:

BNA	Nashville
CVG	Cincinnati
DCA	Washington–National
IAD	Washington–Dulles
EWR	New York–Newark
LGA	New York–La Guardia
IAH	Houston–Intercontinental
ICT	Wichita, Kansas
MCI	Kansas City
MCO	Orlando
MSY	New Orleans
ORD	Chicago–O'Hare
SDF	Louisville, Kentucky
SNA	Orange County, California
YYZ	Toronto

- BEWARE OF TELEPHONE CALLING CARD THIEVES
Watch out for "shoulder surfers" or those that steal your long-distance calling card number by spying on you at airports. Shoulder surfers are more prevalent in cities with large immigrant

populations which provide a perfect market for stolen calling cards. Cover the phone with your body when entering your number, or speak quietly if you must dictate your number to an operator.

- EXPECT DELAYS AT SECURITY CHECKPOINTS DURING CRISES
  Remember the long lines and extra hassles during the Gulf War? Just wait for the next international crisis—it will happen again. Plan on arriving at the airport ahead of time. Expect to see more thermal neutron "scanners" or "sniffers" that will eliminate the need to search bags and help speed up this process. Be sure your electronic gear has working batteries—you'll probably be asked to turn your unit on.

- BE GRATEFUL FOR THE SECURITY INSPECTOR'S VIGILANCE
  Don't hassle your inspector. Proper screening of all passengers could save many lives.

- DON'T PACK GUNS, KNIVES, OR POTENTIAL WEAPONS IN CARRY-ON BAGS
  Believe it or not, people forget that they have weapons in the bottom of their purse or briefcase. Also, toy guns and knives brought home to kids do not amuse security personnel. Best to pack these items in your checked luggage.

- DON'T LEAVE BAGS UNATTENDED
  Unattended bags are prime bomb suspects. Unattended bags on British ferries are thrown overboard or incinerated at Israeli airports.

- MOVE QUICKLY AWAY FROM BOMB SCENES
  In the event of an airport bomb, move away from the scene as quickly as possible—serious terrorists typically plant two bombs—the second as a backup if the first fails.

6

Tips 81-104
On the Plane

FASTEN SEATBELTS

NO SMOKING
NO FUMAR

In his story "Travels with a Donkey," Robert Louis Stevenson claims "For my part, I travel not to go anywhere, but to go. I travel for travel's sake. The great affair is to move." Travel has come a long way since Stevenson's era when beasts of burden were a primary mode of transportation. However, many of us still have a great affair with "moving." These days the preferred mode is jet aircraft. Here are some tips to make those high- altitude moves a little easier:

THE BEST SEATS

| 81 | Most major carriers now reserve "priority seating," or window and aisle seats near the front of the plane for members of their frequent flyer programs. But if available at check-in, gate agents will seat parents traveling with infants in the "bulkhead" or front row seats. Beware of this during the heavy summer or holiday periods. Better bet: ask for an exit row seat where babies aren't allowed. With new FAA regulations, seats by emergency exits or doors have even more legroom than before. These seats are usually only available at check-in. |

| 82 | If you are traveling with someone else and are reserving a seat on a plane with a three-abreast configuration, book the two outer (aisle and window) seats. If the plane is not full, the likelihood of the airline reserving the middle seat is slim. |

| 83 | All planes are not created equal. When an airline orders new planes or refurbishes older ones, the |

airline (not the manufacturer) determines how wide the seats will be and how much legroom they'll allow. Therefore, comfort levels vary from airline to airline.

___

84 In 1993 a reborn TWA removed rows of seats and spaced out remaining seats to provide more legroom. Footrests were installed in coach-class seats on transcontinental and international flights. The move won them "Best Airline for long haul flights" in a December 1993 survey of 24,000 business travelers.

___

85 Smaller domestic carriers Alaska, KIWI, and Midwest Express regularly garner top awards for their extra legroom and in-flight comfort.

___

86 With international first-class cabin occupancy dwindling and business-class sections full, Continental Airlines eliminated first class on international and transcontinental flights and expanded and upgraded the more popular (and affordable) business class, and renamed the hybrid "BusinessFirst." Dutch carrier KLM mimicked the move a few months later. Expect others to follow.

___

87 British Airways offers "sleeper service" in first-class overnight flights from New York. First, passengers are offered dinner on the ground before takeoff. Once on board, the sleeper seats are already made up with cotton sheets, full-sized pillows, and a quilt. Passengers are even offered pajamas.

---

88 | Don't want to be chatted to death by your seat-mate? Put on a set of "Walkman" headphones, even if you are not listening to them.

AIRLINE FOOD

Airline food is a frequent and easy target of business traveler wrath and ridicule. C'mon folks, a stainless steel galley hurtling through the stratosphere at 500 miles per hour is not the most convenient place to pre-pare a dinner banquet for 200. Frankly, it is amazing what some in-flight kitchens can turn out. Most air-lines offer a wide array of unpublicized special meals that are most times an improvement over the standard fare. Requests for special in-flight meals have become de rigueur among many business travelers with restricted diets, or just a taste for something different.

---

89 | Delta's seafood platter is a favorite among fre-quent travelers. American Airlines offers "healthy heart meals" approved by the American Heart Association. United Airlines offers McDonald's "Happy Meals" consisting of cheeseburgers, sausage and biscuits, cookies, and a toy for both adults and children. Arizona-based America West offers Mexican fajitas in first class. Midwest Express Airlines actually bakes chocolate chip cookies in flight and serves them in the aroma-filled cabin.

90 All airlines offer a kosher meal, which is usually fresher and more wholesome than the standard fare. Interestingly, the Moslem meal is usually identical to the kosher meal—only without a rabbi's blessing. The Hindu meal consists of no vegetables that grow beneath the ground and is usually seasoned with curry. Vegetarian meals usually feature whole grain bread, fresh fruit, and vegetables.

Standard list of meal options:

diabetic	low calorie
Hindu	bland
vegetarian Moslem	seafood
nonvegetarian Moslem	child
low/no sodium	lacto-ovo vegetarian
bland	strict vegetarian
low/no fat and cholesterol	fruit

91 Request a special meal through your travel agent or reservationist at least 24 hours before your flight. Since these requests are often overlooked, be sure to follow up on your request by calling ahead on the day of your flight and again at check-in.

92 Flight attendants never seem to be very happy about serving special meals. Be kind. These meals take more time to prepare and more effort to get the right meal to the right person.

93 Your meal options and food quality expand if you can get on the first, or domestic leg of an international flight, that is, a flight from Atlanta to Los Angeles that continues on to Hong Kong. Also, many transcontinental flights have upgraded food offerings.

JET LAG

94 Jet lag can occur on transcontinental or transoceanic flights. Veteran transatlantic travelers usually agree that jet lag is more common after the flight to Europe (eastbound) than after the flight home. The same goes for transpacific flights—your westbound journey there is easier than your eastbound journey home. As a general rule, it takes one day for your body to adjust to each time zone crossed.

95 Flights from the US typically arrive in Europe or Asia early in the morning. Don't plan on conducting too much important business the day you arrive. Instead, use that day to get your circadian rhythms back in sync.

96 The most popular jet lag remedy? Denial. However, avoiding alcohol and regulating your diet and exposure to sunlight are a central theme in the many popular methods for dealing with jet lag. Alcohol consumption compounds your body's confusion and adds to dehydration. Some programs claim that different foods and caffeine used accordingly can help—for energy, eat a high-protein meal and drink coffee. If you want to go to sleep, have a high-carbohydrate meal.

Exposure to as much sunlight as possible at your new destination should help.

---

97 | There is new hope that melatonin, a hormone excreted by the body that helps regulate the sleep–wake cycle can help eliminate jet lag. Studies in England and most recently at Oregon Health Sciences University have shown that an extra dose of melatonin at bedtime at your new destination can help induce a good night's sleep and thereby reset the body's circadian rhythms to the new time zone. Although the application of melatonin in the battle against jet lag is still experimental, FDA approval is expected in the near future.

---

98 | Seventy-nine percent of sleep experts surveyed by the Gallup Organization in 1993 recommend short-acting prescription sleep medications to help their patients sleep on seven to eight-hour night flights. (Ambien, Halcion, and Valium are commonly prescribed.) Homeopathic remedies include camomile tea and aromatherapy.

---

99 | An entire book titled *Overcoming Jet Lag* (Berkley Publishing), has been written on the subject by Dr. Charles Ehret.

---

100 | **Care for Your Ears In Flight**

The rapid changes in altitude and air pressure associated with takeoff and landing can wreak havoc on your inner ear. You can avoid serious problems by following a few simple steps on every flight.

- If you are suffering from a cold or other malady that causes nasal congestion, take a decongestant or nasal spray before your flight. For long flights, take it again about an hour before landing.

- Keep a Vicks (or other) mentholated inhaler in your briefcase when flying during cold and flu season.

- If you feel excess pressure in your ears, open your eustachian tube by yawning or swallowing. If this fails to alleviate the pressure, pinch your nostrils closed and use your cheek and throat muscles to force a mouthful of air against your lips and nostrils. Using your chest and stomach muscles with this maneuver could create too much pressure.

- Chew gum or ice.

- A loud pop in your ears should signal an end to your discomfort. However, if the problem persists, see your physician.

---

101 | Use In-Flight Gadgets to Work and/or Play

In early 1994 most airlines began outfitting aircraft with new digital passenger communications and entertainment systems. These are the first of a new generation of digital (versus analog) in-flight systems. The systems allow passengers to make static-free phone calls, send faxes, transmit computer data, retrieve stock quotes, and play video games—all from a seatback unit, consisting of a viewing screen and a telephone handset with an alphanumeric keypad and game controller buttons, and live news, sports, entertainment, and music radio channels. Soon the system will offer ground-to-air paging, airport gate information, car/hotel/airline reservations, and news/weather headlines.

102 | Know About In-Flight No-Nos

In 1993 the airlines banned the use of laptop computers or CD players during takeoff and landing. Important point: you can still use your laptop once the pilot turns off the seat belt sign and announces that the aircraft has reached cruising altitude. However, you must turn your unit off when the seat belt sign goes back on, signaling descent and landing.

103 | Understand Fear of Flying

If you are a fearful flyer (an "aerophobic"), select a seat at the front of the plane where the ride is smoother and quieter. Talk to the person in the next seat. Recognize that your anxieties are OK but don't focus on them.

What do aerophobics dread most? Crashing and burning top the list. Interestingly, losing control and having to be physically subdued once the plane takes off is the second biggest fear. Other fears include claustrophobia and worrying that the pilot may die of a heart attack and lose control of the aircraft.

Fear of flying is a deep-seated problem that this book alone cannot solve. If the problem persists and threatens your livelihood, call your local Mental Health Association for a list of psychologists that specialize in the treatment of phobias, or try one of the following programs.

- The Pegasus Fear of Flying Foundation, made up of a group of active pilots and practicing psychologists, provides a one-day total immersion program. They provide participants with information about the aviation environment as well as the environment of the mind experiencing phobic fear. Pegasus claims a 100 percent success rate. Call 1-800-FEAR-NOT, or write 200 Eganfuskee St., Jupiter, FL 33477-5068, for more information.

- American Airlines regularly schedules a series of two-day "Fearless Flyer" classes for fearful flyers in various cities around the country. The fee includes a round-trip graduation flight. For information, call 1-800-451-5106.

- Freedom from Fear of Flying, Inc., offers books, seminars, and tapes on the subject. Write 2021 Country Club Prado, Coral Gables, FL 33134, or call (305) 261-7042.

---

104 Play It Safe In Flight (Bonus Tips)

- SIT IN THE REAR OF THE PLANE FOR SAFETY
It is difficult to say where the safest place to sit on a plane is. However, aircraft manufacturers put the "black box" or in-flight recorders in the tail of the plane—the place they feel is least likely to be destroyed in an accident.

- SIT OVER THE WING FOR STABILITY
  If you are prone to motion sickness, a seat over the wing ensures the smoothest ride.

- KEEP SEAT BELT FASTENED AT ALL TIMES
  Even when the pilot says that it's okay to move about the cabin, keep your seat belt fastened. Unexpected turbulence could cause you and anything else in the cabin to hit the ceiling without warning. Keep your seat belt fastened around your hips and below your stomach—so your body will pivot if thrown forward, and the seat belt won't cause internal injury.

- CHOOSE SAFETY-CONSCIOUS AIRLINES WITH NEWER FLEETS
  A survey of airline passengers by the Switzerland-based International Foundation of Airline Passenger Associations (IFAPA) revealed that El Al, Swissair, Lufthansa, Qantas, and Delta are the international carriers perceived as "most safety conscious." During international crises these carriers usually report that their business and first-class bookings remain steady while others decline.

- DON'T PUT HEAVY OR SHARP ITEMS IN THE OVERHEAD BIN
  A laptop computer dropped on your head from a height of six or so feet? Think about it. Heavy items should be stowed underneath the seat in front of you.

- READ THE SAFETY CARD; Listen TO PREFLIGHT ANNOUNCEMENT; PLAN YOUR EXIT

Interviews with air-crash survivors show that reading those "international language" safety cards, mentally noting the nearest exits, and planning an escape route before takeoff were factors in their survival.

- AVOID PROPELLER-DRIVEN AIRCRAFT: FLY JETS, IF POSSIBLE
  The likelihood of a crash is higher on commuter/propeller-driven aircraft. Choose jet service when possible. If you must fly on propeller-driven aircraft, try to avoid bad weather or night flights.

- DON'T TRY TO SNEAK SMOKES IN THE BATHROOM
  Fires from bathroom trash bins have been on the rise ever since the smoking ban went into effect.

CHAPTER 7

Tips 105–120
On the Road:
Renting/Driving Cars

You've made it through the friendly skies. Now it's time to get on the road. Whether you rent a car in conjunction with a flight, or you drive your own car on business, this chapter is for you.

At the Car Rental Counter

| 105 | How to get the best car? Ask for the car with the least mileage. Counter agents have mileage information on their computer screens.

| 106 | You don't have to accept the car the agent chooses for you. This is especially true for weekly or longer rentals. Check out your car before you drive it off the lot. If you are dissatisfied, ask for another one. If you don't like the smell of smoke, request a nonsmoking car.

| 107 | According to industry convention, car rental agencies cannot downgrade you if they do not have a car of the size you reserved. They must upgrade you at no additional cost, and if they don't have any larger cars, they should send you to a competitor and pay any difference in the rate applied.

| 108 | Most car rental companies have more large cars than small ones. By reserving a compact car at a cheap rate, the chances are that when you arrive and a compact is not available, you'll be upgraded to a larger car, free of charge.

109 Always mention your affiliation with organizations such as the American Automobile Association or most other motor clubs, American Small Business Association, National Association for the Self-Employed, The Red Cross, or others for automatic discounts of 10 percent or more.

110 For cheaper rates, check with "off-airport" operators. Car rental companies that don't have to pay stiff airport taxes and fees for "on-airport" sites can afford to charge you less. Important point: Be sure you have directions on how to get back to the off-airport lot to return the car. Many off-airport lots are very difficult to find, and usually in desolate, if not dangerous neighborhoods.

111 Warning: You could be denied a car rental (at the counter, not when making your reservation) if your license has been suspended or if your driving record shows that within the last three years you have been charged with: driving under the influence of alcohol or drugs, reckless driving that resulted in bodily injury or property damage, had two or more accidents, driving without proof of insurance, or failing to report an accident. New tracking programs allow car rental companies to access a growing number of state DMV records.

112 Don't fall for the agent's hard sell on their different "refueling options." (Most preposterous: "prepurchase a tank of gas and bring the car back empty!" Driving around a strange city on a low tank of gas? No, thanks.) Be safe and save money by allotting enough time to stop and fill up the car yourself before returning it.

DRIVING TIPS

| 113 | Invest in a car phone or rent one if you are renting a car. Some car rental companies will give you a phone—you only pay for the calls you make. A recent Gallup study found that people who use car phones find travel less stressful. Also, a car phone is an excellent safety feature.

| 114 | Make driving a learning experience. Listen to books on cassette when on road trips. Popular topics include self-help, fiction, and business. Tapes cost $10 to $15 and are available at most bookstores and record stores.

| 115 | Don't rent if you are only going to drive to your hotel and park. Consider your options: a free hotel shuttle, cab, limo, or public transportation (see Chapter 4). If you are renting for only short trips, ask about a cheaper rate with a mileage cap of 100 or so miles per day.

| 116 | If you regularly rent cars, consider joining one of the "frequent renter" programs like Hertz #1 Gold, or National's Emerald Aisle. This way you avoid a lot of the usual car rental hassles like waiting in lines to check in or check out. They also offer upgrades and other perks.

| 117 | The 1994 official IRS-approved per-mile driving rate is 29 cents. That is the amount you can deduct from your taxes for the miles you logged on business. The 29-cent standard mileage rate includes the cost of insurance, license and registration, depreciation, fuel, oil, tires, and maintenance.

| 118 | For international travelers, US state-issued driver's licenses are valid in many countries. If you aren't sure call the American Automobile Association (AAA). They can issue you an international driver's permit for $10. Inquire about the type of car you will be renting—many foreign locations rent only cars with manual transmissions. Check with your insurance company or credit card company before you go to determine coverages.

| 119 | Understand Insurance Issues

- Don't buy the $7 to $13 per day Collision Damage Waiver (CDW) protection. Your personal insurance, your company insurance, or your credit card will cover you in most cases. However, some car insurance companies and credit card companies are quietly pulling their automatic collision and liability coverage for those who rent cars for business purposes. Be sure to call your insurance provider and credit card company periodically to check on this protection.

- Ask your credit card company if they provide *primary* or *secondary* coverage. *Secondary* coverage protects you only if your personal policy does not. The problem with secondary coverage is that in many cases, you may still be responsible for the deductible amount on your personal insurance, and of course, you can expect a rate increase.

- Remember that credit card companies provide collision coverage, not liability coverage. Recently, most major car rental companies changed their contracts to make the renter's liability policy (typically part of their personal or company auto insurance coverage) the first line of defense in an accident involving a liability claim. If you don't own a car and/or have no other liability coverage, you'll face problems if you are involved in an accident that damages property or kills or injures someone. (Nonowners should consider the car rental company's expensive daily liability coverage.)

120 | Play It Safe on the Road (Bonus Tips)

- DRIVING IS 70 PERCENT TO 100 PERCENT MORE DANGEROUS THAN FLYING
Some airlines like to remind you of this in their landing announcements: "Now that the safest part of your journey is over. . ."

- CARRY A SPARE TIRE AND CHECK IT PERIODICALLY
Newer American cars have those hard-rubber, tiny replacement tires to use when you have a flat. Older cars and some European/Japanese models still have an inflatable spare. Be sure that it is inflated.

- CARRY A ROADSIDE EMERGENCY KIT
  These kits typically include basic tools, flares, a flashlight, and some first aid supplies. They can be real life savers.

- CARRY AN UP-TO-DATE MAP; ASK FOR DIRECTIONS BEFORE LEAVING THE LOT
  Always request a map at the rental car counter. And always get good directions to your hotel from the airport. Most crimes directed at drivers happen to those that are lost. Ask rental agents which areas of town to avoid.

- AVOID PARKING RENTAL CARS WITH OUT-OF-STATE TAGS OR OTHER IDENTIFYING FEATURES IN UNGUARDED LOTS
  These cars shout "trunk full of goodies" to thieves. However, the recent rash of crimes directed at cars with rental company markings has forced most companies to remove them in most states. Another good idea—don't rent an inexpensive hatchback model if you are planning on storing things in your car.

- AVOID CAR JACKING
  Keep your luggage and other valuables in the trunk and out of sight. Keep your purse or briefcase on the floor—never on the front passenger seat. Keep at least one car length between you and the car in front of you when stopping. This prevents you from being blocked in and unable to get away if car jackers drive up behind you. If another car bumps you, if someone yells, honks, or points at your car as if there was something

wrong, or if a driver flashes his headlights at you, *do not stop*. Drive to the nearest well-lit, populated place, then investigate. (Another good time to use a car phone.)

- DON'T PICK UP HITCHHIKERS
  Just like your mother told you.

- DON'T USE UNOFFICIAL ROADS
  Especially in foreign countries.

CHAPTER 8

Tips 121–135
At the Hotel

A hotel stay is a key part of most business trips—and all business travelers have endured as many hotel stays as they have enjoyed. Some hotels stays are memorable, some you try to forget, and some just blend into that one big beige hotel experience in the back of your mind.

These days hotels are hurting more than ever, and business travelers are running into some unpleasant surprises. Complaints range from longer lines at check-in and check-out and abbreviated room service hours, to worn furnishings and spotty amenities. But with overbuilding and less demand, hotels are fighting tooth and nail to retain their customers and stay in business. Business travelers may now enjoy greater clout, but they might have to put up with poorer service. In this chapter we try to help you find a happy medium.

GETTING THE BEST RATE

121 You can almost always get a better deal by calling the hotel directly instead of a central 800 reservations line. Sometimes by simply asking "Is this the lowest rate available?" can net big savings. Hotels have caught on to the airlines' practice of "yield management," which means that a hotel room that is worth X today could be worth Y tomorrow. So if at first you don't succeed, keep trying.

122 A generic "corporate rate" is not always the best deal. If your company does not have a special rate, ask for the rate of the company you are visiting (even if they are a prospective client). Many times the hotel's local sales office has set up a special "private" rate that only in-house reservationists are aware of. (However, desk clerks are more likely to upgrade a traveler on a corporate rate than a discount rate.)

---

123 Ask for association discounts. Membership in the American Automobile Association (AAA), the American Association of Retired Persons (AARP), or other national organizations can sometimes net discounts.

---

124 If you plan to stay at a specific hotel for an extended period, arrange a meeting with a member of the hotel sales staff to negotiate the best rate possible. Shop around. Most hotels are eager to snare long-term business.

---

125 Beware of hidden charges and taxes. New York City hotels charge a whopping 21.25 percent tax on all rooms over $100. Also check ahead of time on extras that can add up, like incoming fax charges, per call telephone charges, or hefty parking fees when driving. Staying at a hotel that limits these add-ons can help save money.

---

126 Inquire about the relatively new "business-class" rooms (with services like free local calls and long-distance access, in-room fax, coffeemaker, newspaper, etc.) for one package price. Within the past year, Hilton, Guest Quarters, Radisson, Hyatt, and Clarion have tested variations of this concept in many properties. It's a great idea for those who feel nickel and dimed to death at the checkout counter. Ask about these rooms when you make your reservation.

127 If you will be working in your hotel room during the summer, don't forget to request a room away from the shrieks and squeals of the hotel pool area.

128 Try hotel consolidators who purchase hotel room blocks then resell them at deep discounts. They do not charge for the service; however, many require that you pay in advance with a credit card. Try the Hotel Reservations Network: 800-964-6835; or Quikbook at 800-221-3531.

129 Many travel agents band together with others to obtain volume-based discounts from individual and chain hotels. Always ask your travel agent to find you a *consortium* rate.

130 Desperate? If you are stuck in a strange city with no reservation, and can't find a room, ask the desk clerk or manager about the possibility of placing a rollaway bed in a meeting room for the night. If available, use the hotel health club to shower.

WHEN THINGS GO WRONG

131 What to do when you arrive at your hotel after a long journey, and the perky young desk clerk tells

you that although you have a confirmed reservation (evidenced by the reservation confirmation
number you are holding in your hand) there are
no rooms available? The hotels have caught on to
the airlines' practice of overbooking, and in their
lingo, when there is no room available, the guest
is walked. If this happens to you, ask for:

1. A free long-distance telephone call to notify
   office or family of your hotel change.
2. Free transportation to a nearby comparable
   hotel.
3. The offending hotel should pay for your first
   night at the nearby hotel.

Some hotels will offer you free upgrade certificates of free weekend vouchers too. Remember
that you must ask for these things, otherwise you
may not get them.

---

132 | Tips for Calling from Your Hotel Room:

- Always ask what the fee for calling card access is
  when you check in. If you plan to make several
  calls, you may choose to stay elsewhere. If you
  have no alternatives, you can always use the pay
  phone in the hotel lobby.

- If you are making a series of long distance
  calls, hit the # sign between calls (don't hang up)
  for a new dial tone. Per-call fees stack up when
  you hang up and reenter your credit card number
  over and over.

- Complain to the hotel manager about the fees. If they are particularly outrageous, ask that they be removed from your bill.

(Find more tips in Chapter 9, Using the Phone)

---

133 | Hotels listen to customers who complain. Over the past few years, hotels have completely revamped their offerings to attract more business travelers. Business travelers account for up to 70 percent of all hotel guests. It is up to you to let hoteliers know how they are doing.

What to do if you feel you are not getting proper service at a hotel? Stan Bromley, general manager of the Four Seasons, Washington, advises: "You complain—you send it back. A New Yorker in a deli either enjoys what he gets or he won't accept it. The same should apply to hotel stays—if it is not up to par, send it back and don't pay for it. To complain, call the manager or the manager's secretary."

---

134 | **Understand How the Hotel Industry Is Organized**

Over the last decade, the hotel industry has become "segmented." It is important for business travelers to know what each segment means and where they fit in. Some major hotel chains like Marriott and Choice International offer a hotel product in each segment. Others, like the Four Seasons or Budgetel, specialize in a single segment.

- LUXURY

  These hotels cater to those looking for personalized services, fine dining restaurants, in-room
  business services, 24-hour room service, and posh
  fitness centers or spas. Special privileges and
  pampering make these hotels unique. Luxury
  chains with a major presence in the US include
  Four Seasons and Ritz-Carlton. Several independent hotels and smaller chains affiliated with
  marketing groups like "Preferred Hotels,"
  "Leading Hotels of the World," or "Relais and
  Chateaux" also fall into the luxury category.
  Typical guests include high-ranking corporate
  officers, successful entrepreneurs, and the inde-
  pendently wealthy.

- QUALITY OR UPSCALE

  Quality hotels have a diverse clientele ranging
  from conventioneers and business travelers to
  vacationing families. These full service hotels
  are popular due to services and amenities like
  frequent stay programs, meeting space, room
  service, business centers, express check-in/check-
  out, and fitness clubs. These hotels usually have
  concierge levels that offer "luxury" hotel services—typically a lounge offering free breakfasts
  and cocktail hours and a separate check-in area.
  Guests traveling on business are mostly mid-
  to upper-level managers and salespeople, incen-
  tive groups, and some conventions. Chains
  include Swissôtel, Inter-Continental, Westin,
  Stouffer, Nikko, Omni, Hilton, and Hyatt,
  Sheraton, and Marriott.

- MODERATE

  These hotels are most widely used by business travelers because of cost and convenience. Most offer a good location, several food and beverage options, meeting space, video in-room check-out, and exercise rooms. Because the services offered by these hotels can range from just under luxury hotel standards to just above economy hotel standards, it is a good idea to find out a little bit about the hotel before making a long-term reservation. Holiday Inn, Radisson, Ramada Inn, Days Inn, and Howard Johnson are some examples.

- ECONOMY

  These limited service hotels are attractive to independent business travelers, those on a per diem, or corporations geared toward reducing travel budgets. These hotels offer few amenities, but most offer a clean, comfortable room. Most do not have a restaurant on the premises, but you'll now find many sharing a parking lot (and a symbiotic relationship) with a family style or fern bar (like Bennigans, TGI Fridays) type restaurant. Chains include Budgetel, Hampton Inns, Fairfield Inns, Red Roof, Comfort Inns, La Quinta, Holiday Inn Express, Days Inn, and Econo-Lodges.

- EXTENDED STAY

  These suite hotels are most popular with people relocating to a new city, attending a training program, or on a temporary assignment. Their home-like features include: kitchens, fireplaces, shopping services, complimentary breakfast, and weekly guest gatherings. Rates depend on how long the guest stays—most decrease significantly after the first 7–10 days. Chains include Residence Inn by Marriott, Hilton Suites, Guest Quarters, Summerfield Suites, and Embassy Suites.

- Increasingly popular alternatives to impersonal, run-of-the-mill hotels in all categories are lesser-known boutique hotels or bed and breakfast establishments. With more personalized service and a more secure atmosphere, many female business travelers have become bed and breakfast regulars. Ask about these "finds" by calling local chambers of commerce, convention and visitor's bureaus, or by word of mouth.

---

135 | Play It Safe in Your Hotel (Bonus Tips)

- CHECK OUT HOTEL LOCATION PRIOR TO THE TRIP
  Ask your travel agent, or someone from the city where you are going about the hotel's neighborhood. If you are in a questionable area, ask a hotel employee to park your car for you. Also, the hotel should provide escorts to the parking lots. If you are an exercise buff, ask about the safest areas to jog or run. When on the road, try to run in the morning or at lunch—avoid outdoor workouts when it is dark.

- KNOW FIRE ESCAPE/SURVIVAL PROCEDURES
  Just like air crash survivors, hotel fire survivors report that they had their escape route mapped out before the fire alarm went off. Just take a

quick look at the diagram on the back of your door. In case of a fire: If there is no fire in the hallway, head to the exit, taking your room key. If you sense heat and smoke, stay low. If stuck in your room, fill the bathtub with water, soak towels, call the front desk to report the fire and your whereabouts. To help firefighters locate you, open or remove the drapes from your window, write HELP on the glass using shaving cream, soap, or whatever is available. Breathe through a moistened washcloth.

- USE HOTEL SAFES FOR VALUABLES
Don't try to hide valuables in your room. An experienced burglar will find any hiding place you create. Store jewelry, cash, electronics, or other valuables in an in-room safe or hotel safe deposit box.

- STAY ON THE THIRD THROUGH SIXTH FLOOR
Burglars are more likely to target rooms on the lower levels, and firefighting equipment doesn't always reach above the sixth.

- HANG THE DO NOT DISTURB SIGN AND LEAVE THE TV ON WHEN OUT
Never leave the MAID PLEASE sign on the door—call housekeeping and ask them to have your room cleaned instead.

- VERIFY ROOM DELIVERIES WITH THE FRONT DESK OR ROOM SERVICE

- HOTEL SAFETY FEATURES TO INQUIRE ABOUT WHEN MAKING YOUR RESERVATION:

  - Well-lit interior hallways with monitored entrances. It is easier to secure rooms in hotels with one or two monitored entrances. Motels with exterior doors in unattended areas are prime targets.
  - Electronic door locks. It's impossible to duplicate keys—codes are changed after each guest checks out.
  - At least three bolts, locks or chains, and peepholes on hotel room doors. Your door should have a dead bolt, a chain, and a regular door lock. Be sure all three are secure before going to bed. Some business travelers pack the small brown rubber wedges typically used to keep doors open. In this case, the wedge is placed behind the closed door to prevent forced entry.

Tips 136–148
Using the Telephone

The telephone is without question the most-used tool of the business traveler. Communication options by telephone have expanded in the last decade—so much so that a simple long-distance call has become confusing to many.

Here are some ways to be sure that you are getting the biggest bang for your telephone bucks.

FROM HOTEL PHONES OR PAY PHONES

Typically, a traveling salesperson must make a series of long-distance calls each night to report back on the day's sales activity, to call the boss or co-worker, to set up future appointments, or to call home. Access fees from in-room phones vary widely, from free to $1.25 nationwide. This fee is no problem when the traveler makes one or two calls a night. But when several calls are made, these charges can really stack up.

| 136 | Chainwide, Stouffer Hotel guests are charged only for local calls. All 800 and long-distance access fees are waived. As this book went to print, Hilton Hotels announced their "Free Access" policy, which eliminates fees for guests making calling card calls at 65 "participating" Hilton properties. A Hilton spokesman said that the rest of the hotel's 200+ properties should follow suit. Other major hotel chains may be forced to drop the lucrative fees universally now that Hilton, one of the industry's largest players, announced this policy.

137 Always use a credit card when making long-distance calls. Direct-dialed calls from your room are typically assessed at a 40 percent premium. To avoid outrageous surcharges for using your hotel room phone, access your long-distance carrier directly by dialing one of the following numbers:

1-0-2-8-8-0 or (800) 3210-ATT for AT&T
1-0-2-2-2-0 or (800) 950-1022 for MCI
1-0-3-3-3-0 or (800) 877-8000 for Sprint

138 New Federal Communications Commission (FCC) rules require hotels and pay phones to allow access to all long-distance carriers. Problems? Report them to the FCC Enforcement Division, Common Carrier Bureau, 2025 M Street, Washington, DC, 20554.

139 When making a series of credit card calls from your hotel room, don't hang up between calls. Hit the # sign for a new dial tone between calls to avoid an individual fee for each call. Fees stack up when you hang up and reenter your credit card number over and over.

140 Always ask what the fee for calling card access is when you check in. If you plan to make several calls, you may choose to stay elsewhere. If worst comes to worst, use the pay phone in the hotel lobby. If you are stuck with a bill that you feel is unfair, complain to the manager. Request that it be reduced or eliminated.

FROM ANY PHONE

---

141 Did you know that every time you make a calling card call with most major carriers, you are charged a 60-cent to 80-cent surcharge in addition to toll charges? However, smaller telecommunications companies (found in your phone book) and resellers offer no-surcharge calling cards.

---

142 Did you know that with some (not all) calling cards you can assign an accounting code to each call, making reimbursement among multiple clients much easier? Ask about this feature when you sign up. It is usually free.

---

143 The latest trend to sweep the long-distance telephone market: *debit cards*. (Remember, a free one from MCI with this book.) You buy a debit card with a specific dollar value ($10, $25, $50), call the 800 number listed on the card, enter a PIN code, and make calls nationwide at a flat rate. When the time is used up, you throw the card away. Debit cards are good for: limiting your exposure if the card number is stolen; giving a set amount of long distance to traveling employees, college students, colleagues, customers or friends; giving as a premium to customers or potential clients. The biggest drawback with debit cards has been cost. Until recently, companies offering debit cards charged a prohibitive 50 cents to 60 cents per minute. However, some companies are offering debit cards for as little as 33 cents per minute. That means that it is cheaper to use a debit card than it is to make a credit card call—because you avoid those 60 cent to 80 cent per-call surcharges.

BONUS TIP: To save time, save money, and preserve your peace of mind, set up a telephone call schedule with your office and with your family. For example, let your office know that you'll call in for messages every day at 1:15 PM or that you'll call your family every Tuesday and Thursday at 7 PM.

---

144 | Consider Personal 800 Services

The explosion of new technology and new phone service providers has brought the cost of 800 service down to the personal level. You may want to consider personal 800 service if:

- You, your spouse, or your children frequently call home from out of town.

- You call your answering machine several times a day to check for messages.

- You stay at hotels that charge access fees for connection to long-distance services, but not 800 numbers.

- Your long-distance carrier charges per-call "set-up" fees on credit card calls. (Most charge 50 cents to 90 cents minimum per call.)

The personal 800 services of the major phone companies charge around $5.00 per month and 20 cents to 25 cents per call. Service set-up fees range from $0 to $10. Smaller telecommunications companies and resellers offer even better packages.

Important points: 800 service runs through your existing phone lines. And you don't have to change your current long-distance carrier to get the 800 service from another carrier.

INTERNATIONAL CALLING

145 Sometimes outrageous hotel surcharges and local taxes can add up to more than the cost of the call itself. If you know that you will be making a lot of long-distance calls on a trip overseas, call your long-distance carrier before you go and ask about AT&T's "USA Direct," MCI's "Call USA," or Sprint's "Express" services. Once outside North America, you simply dial your carrier's local access number from any phone in the country, which connects you automatically to an operator in the US. The operator places the call back to the US or to another country for you. (Country-to-country calling can be limited with some cards—best to check ahead of time.) Charges appear on your home or office phone bill—not your hotel bill. To dial the special access number, your hotel will typically charge you for only a local call. A few charge a premium.

146 If you plan to make a lot of local or domestic long-distance calls from public phones while in another country, consider buying a phone debit card from a post office or newsstand in many cities around the world. This way, you just insert the card into a public phone and dial away, instead of fumbling through your pockets for unfamiliar foreign coins. Although a relatively unknown concept here, the phone debit card is widely used overseas for both domestic and international calls.

---

147 Many countries outside North America do not have Touch-Tone systems, but many US-based travelers' answering machines and voice mail systems require tones to retrieve messages. Solution: Electronics stores (like Radio Shack) provide "tone generators," pocket-sized gadgets that emit a tone into the phone mouthpeice.

---

148 Watch out for "shoulder surfers" or people who steal your long-distance calling card number by spying on you at airports or train and bus stations, then sell the number on the street. Shoulder surfers are more prevalent in cities with large immigrant populations—perfect markets for stolen calling card numbers. Insert your calling card in phones that allow it, or cover the phone with your body when entering your number. Speak quietly if you must dictate you number to an operator.

CHAPTER 10

Tips 149–157
Frequent Traveler Programs

There are three milestones in the history of the airline industry. The first of course is the Orville and Wilbur Wright story. Second, the introduction of commercial jet aircraft in the 1960s. The third is no doubt the launch of frequent traveler programs in 1981. In the years since, this marketing phenomenon has become firmly entrenched in the travel industry spreading beyond the airlines to hotel chains, car rental companies, cruise lines, and credit cards. As of 1994 over 32 million frequent travelers had earned over 1.3 billion miles—roughly 61,000 domestic round-trip tickets. And after years of looking down their noses at them, most international carriers now offer frequent traveler programs. So for better or for worse, it looks as though the programs are here to stay.

The appeal of frequent traveler programs is obvious— free travel, airline, hotel, car upgrades, and more respect at the ticket counter, to name a few. But staying on top of each program, tracking your miles, sifting through endless statements, program newsletters, and advertisements, and even finding time to take the free trips are frustrations that all frequent travelers endure.

Some tips to help you wade through this growing milieu.

---

149 | Concentrate on One or Two Programs

- By concentrating on just a few programs, members more easily attain the much sought after "elite" status. Elite members (usually in the top 10 percent of flyers) are today's true "frequent" travelers. Anyone can sign up for a frequent flyer program, but it is the elite members that the airlines really recognize and reward.

- Concentrate on one, but go ahead and sign up for as many programs as you can—almost all are free. You never know when you may end up on an airline or in a hotel that you rarely use. Think about what happens when planes get rerouted, when you get bumped from your flight or hotel. If you aren't signed up, you won't accumulate miles. Also, when you are signed up for many programs, you'll be on their mailing lists, so you'll hear about new offers, new service, or occasional bonuses. To get program applications, see your travel agent or take a walk through the airport and pick up applications from the ticket counters.

- Decide which programs you want to concentrate on. In many cities like Pittsburgh, Atlanta, Houston, Dallas, Miami, or other "fortress hub" cities, your frequent flyer program "decision" is moot. For those living in cities with more diverse choices, or those in hub cities choosing a secondary airline, take these questions into consideration:

  - Do you want free trips to international destinations? Some airlines have better international networks or program partners than others.

  - Do you prefer to use your awards for upgrades? Some programs are much more liberal with upgrades than others.

- How about merchandise awards? For those who would rather not get on another plane to use their awards, some airlines offer better merchandise programs than others.

- Who will use your awards? Delta restricts the transferability of awards to family members only. All the other airlines allow members to transfer the awards to anyone they choose.

- When do you plan to redeem your miles? Award time limits vary. Some airlines' miles expire after two or three years. Some don't.

- Who are the airline's partners? Proper management of partner hotel, car rental, and credit card programs can help add 20 percent to 30 percent to your annual mileage bottom line.

---

150 | Aim for Elite Levels

- Again, choosing a program or two to concentrate on will get you to the elite levels of membership much faster. Most airlines offer basic elite membership to those members who fly as little as 25,000 miles per year.

- The airlines award elite membership for *base miles flown*, not miles earned. This means that the points you earn in bonus programs or partner programs will not help you get into elite levels.

- As airlines try to attract the true "creme de la creme," elite levels are establishing new hierarchies. For example, Continental awards bronze, silver, and gold levels of elite membership. Delta recently launched "Royal Medallion" (versus normal Medallion) status for members flying over 60,000 base miles per year. In late 1993, TWA unveiled its "Royal Ambassador" level.

- Elite level programs vary slightly, but most offer special reservations telephone numbers; a priority waiting list on full flights; first class check-in; priority baggage handling; preferred coach seating (aisle and window seats near the front); special menu selection; liberal upgrade policies; per flight and "plateau" mileage bonuses (the rich get richer, faster!); and limited blackout days for free travel.

151 | Use Your Points to Upgrade

The ability to upgrade is probably the most cherished benefit of frequent flyer programs. There are three main avenues frequent flyers should use to move into the comfort and space of the first-class cabin.

- Cash in your miles for upgrade certificates to be used for confirmed first-class seats. Most airlines require at least 10,000 miles. These certificates provide the most value when you are taking a long haul transcontinental or international flight.

- Elite level upgrades. Some airlines offer elite members the opportunity to upgrade to first class on a space available basis at the gate. Others require elite members to call ahead. Still others will mail out upgrade certificates to be used at the gate or when you make your reservation. Confirmed upgrades are, of course, the most valuable—especially for those Friday afternoon flights when every frequent flyer is hovering around the gate flashing plastic and vying for standby upgrades.

- Purchased upgrades. For frequent travelers flying on certain fares, most airlines provide the opportunity to purchase an upgrade for significantly less than the price of a true first-class ticket. The price of the upgrade depends on the length of the flight. Still other airlines will confirm a first-class seat for members paying full-coach or unrestricted fares.

---

152 | Plan Ahead

- After chosing your primary airline, decide on an award goal. Then decide where you want to go and when you want to go. Don't forget that there are millions of other frequent flyers who want to fly free to Europe in the summer and to Hawaii in the winter. There are also millions of others who are willing to pay for a seat to these desirable destinations. As you may expect, the airlines have capacity controls on the number of free tickets they give away to these destinations.

- When making your reservation for a free trip, try to have alternate dates in mind. Otherwise, you may have to plan 3 to 15 months ahead of time to get the exact itinerary you want. Most airline programs have blackout dates around holidays and peak travel periods. Some programs offer the opportunity to redeem fewer miles if you can travel at off-peak times ("mileage saver" or "mileage stretcher" plans). Off-peak usually means traveling to warm places in the summer and cold places in the winter, or flying Tuesday, Wednesday, or Thursday. The two best months for free travel: October or May. The two worst: December and January.

- If the flights you want aren't available, ask to be put on the waiting list. Or call back. Plans change, flight inventories change, so a flight that's full this week could have an open seat next week or next month.

| 153 | **Stay Up to Date**

- Fierce competition for the loyalty of the business traveler has the airline programs offering a rapidly changing array of perks and promotions. Industrywide financial instability has program partners bowing in and bowing out at least yearly.

- Read your mail as often as you can. If nothing else, read the newsletter of your chosen airline program. Read *InsideFlyer*, *USA TODAY*'s Money section, or *Frequent Flyer Magazine* (see Chapter 2). There you'll find out about special bonus programs, segment promotions, double or triple miles to certain cities, upgrade opportunities, mileage discounts for free travel, partnership promotions, and so forth.

- At least once a year, sit down with your statement and a current awards chart to see where you stand. Award requirements change as often as fares. Plus, you'll see if you can travel at certain times or to or through certain cities to earn bonus miles.

---

154 | Beware of Expiring Miles

- Miles earned on United, American, America West, Northwest, and Alaska Airlines expire after three years. (In 1992 American purged almost 9 billion expired mileage points from its program.) However, miles earned before the mileage expiration policies went into effect (in 1988) do not expire.

- Currently US Air, Delta, Continental, and TWA have no expiration dates on their miles. But this liability on the books in a worsening airline economic environment could mean expiring miles sooner instead of later.

---

155 | Use Partner Programs

- You can substantially add to your total miles and points annually by properly choosing and using the airlines' hotel, rental car, credit card, and phone card partners.

- Hotel frequent stay programs are not nearly as popular as the frequent flyer programs, but offer excellent benefits like upgrades to concierge levels, free morning papers, check-cashing privileges, premium rooms, and so forth. Most hotel programs operate on number or "stays" versus number of nights. The best hotel programs offer very generous merchandise rewards as well as free travel. Like the airline programs, elite levels within hotel programs (for as few as 15 stays per year) are worth aiming for too.

• In 1993 most major hotels revamped or added programs that allow you to earn airline miles for hotel stays—not necessarily in conjunction with flights. Marriott, Sheraton, Holiday Inn, and Hilton and Hyatt announced new programs stressing air miles. With these programs, travelers must choose whether they want to earn airline miles or hotel program points, not both. Hilton and Westin are the only exceptions, still allowing "double dipping" or earning both hotel points and airline miles.

• Your mileage goal is much more easily reached using partners—but remember that miles earned from partners won't count as the base miles necessary for elite status.

---

156 | Seek Help

• To the harried frequent traveler's rescue is Randy Petersen, perhaps the nation's most authoritative voice when it comes to these programs. Petersen is the owner of Colorado Springs-based Frequent Flyer Services (FFS), which offers three helpful tools to program members:

– They publish *InsideFlyer*, a monthly magazine that tracks the programs and helps travelers stay on top of the ever changing promotions, bonuses, awards, information, and advice.

- Many of Petersen's tips, as well as charts explaining 53 frequent traveler programs, are compiled in his annual *Official Frequent Flyer Guidebook* (AirPress, $14.99).

- To help frequent travelers maintain an accurate accounting of the points and credits accumulated in all their programs, FFS tracks individual programs for members. They also offer insurance on members' mileage banks if an airline were to default. Information: 800-333-5937.

---

157 | Plan for the Future

- In late 1993 the Internal Revenue Service reaffirmed that airlines do not have to report the frequent flyer miles awarded to passengers because they are unable to determine if the awards result in gross income to the recipients. With little support for the idea and the possibility of a bookkeeping nightmare, analysts expect the IRS to continue to steer clear of the programs as a potential source of revenue.

- Many of the major US carriers (those with the strongest programs) are downsizing their fleets, buying smaller planes, and cutting back on flight frequencies. That means fewer seats and even fewer "free" seats allotted for frequent travelers, making proper frequent travel program management all the more important.

Tips 158–169
International Travel

Working or traveling overseas on business used to be the domain of "career expatriates"—you know, the James Bond international affairs types, probably not the best managers in the home office, but too smart or well connected to let go. These were the ones sent overseas.

Now US companies, saddled with slow growth or saturated markets at home, are taking their international markets much more seriously. Faced with stiff competition from internationally savvy and powerful foreign companies, US companies are sending their smartest, brightest, and even youngest on overseas assignments.

With the exception of Japan, we are about the only population that refers to travel outside our borders as "going overseas." Americans grow up without the easy cultural exchanges and experiences that those dwelling in most world regions can experience over a weekend or in an easy commute. The result is that we seldom go overseas prepared to understand, accept, or accommodate the workplace of a host country. Many learn the hard way the "American way" is not the only way. Other nationalities are more accustomed to recognizing and accommodating the "ugly American" than we are of returning the favor.

An overseas assignment no longer means months or years abroad. With a shrinking world, it is now common for some managers to dart off to the other side of the world for a short time. Indeed, there is a small but growing number of business travelers who ply the north Atlantic every week and consider it a "commute."

For international travel to truly be a feather in the cap of a rising star, the trip must be successful. This chapter offers some general tips to take into consideration before you head out over the Atlantic, Pacific, Caribbean, or just across the border to Canada or Mexico. This chapter covers the basics, but in international travel, specifics are important. Before you embark on any trip abroad, read up on the minutiae. There are many good guidebooks, but don't discount a good book (like a Clavell novel for travel to Asia), a recent newspaper from the country where you are going, or a detailed magazine article.

Tips for Your Trip

158 | Complete Your Paperwork

- In 1993 new passports, good for 10 years, cost $65. Renewals cost $55. For up-to-date information, ask your travel agent, or call the State Department's information line at 202-647-0518. If applying for a passport for the first time, you must apply in person at a passport agency or post office to fill out your application and pay your fee. You need to bring proof of US citizenship (i.e., a certified copy of a birth certificate or a certificate of naturalization or citizenship); two identical, recent, 2"x 2" front-view photographs with a light background (many post offices will now take your picture on site), and proof of identity—a valid driver's license is sufficient.

- To renew your passport, fill out a renewal form, which you can get from most post offices or travel agencies, and send it to the passport agency address on the form with your old passport, two new 2"x 2" front-view photos, and a $55 check. Your new passport will be mailed to you. (Tip: If you are sentimentally attached to your old passport, it will be invalidated and returned to you.)

- The passport office is busiest from March through June. If you apply for your passport during this time, allow several weeks for delivery to avoid unecessary delays. However, should you need a passport (or visa) pronto, your travel agent should be able to connect you with services that can help speed up the sometimes lengthy application process. For $50 to $200, these services walk your application through the issuing offices in one to five days. All you have to do is express mail your completed application (available at post offices or courthouses) and two photographs to them.

- Know the difference between a passport and a visa. When the US government gives you a passport, it is providing only a document that permits you to leave the United States. A visa is an official authorization stamped within the passport that permits travel within a country for a specified purpose and a limited time. It is a good idea to contact the country's embassy or consulate closest to you for the most up-to-date information on visa requirements. Visa requirements are sometimes politically charged and can change with the change of government.

- In some countries, your contracts may be null and void if you signed them while traveling on the wrong type of visa. You could even run into problems expensing your trip with the IRS.

---

159 | Plan Ahead

- For business travelers with computer modems, the new, free (except for the cost of the long-distance call to Washington) Consular Affairs Bulletin Board provides up-to-the-minute information on security alerts, passports, visas, medical requirements, and other international travel matters. Information can be downloaded and printed for distribution to fellow travelers. Users of any IBM compatible or Apple computer equipped with a modem can log on by calling 202-647-9225.

- If you don't have a modem, you can call the State Department's Citizen's Emergency Center at 202-647-5225 for a full menu of 24-hour-a-day recordings of all current travel advisories accessed by pushing the buttons on your phone.

- Keep the street address and telephone number of the US embassy or consulate in the city where you are going in your wallet, separate from your passport.

- Before leaving, empty your wallet on to a photocopier and copy your credit cards, driver's license, and other essential documents. Also, copy your plane ticket, your passport and/or visa. Store these documents separately. If you ever lose your wallet or plane ticket, you will be eternally grateful for heeding this advice.

• Know the emergency assistance numbers provided by your credit card company (American Express's number is 202-783-7474) or travel agency. These numbers can be called collect for help on finding emergency medical or legal help overseas. Check with your insurance company to determine the limits of their coverage overseas. This goes for health, life, and car insurance.

160 | Stay Healthy

Becoming ill at home is an inconvenience. Becoming ill overseas can be a nightmare. The best advice we can give is to prevent mishaps by planning ahead.

• Get a checkup. Be sure that you are well enough to take a trip. Sometimes overlooked, but equally important—get a dental checkup.

• Check with the State Department 202-647-5225; the Centers for Disease Control 404-639-2572; or consult your local public health department to find out what vaccines or immunizations are needed or recommended for the countries you will be traveling. For the most part, you will not need any shots for trips to developed countries.

- Bring an ample supply of your prescription drugs. You cannot rely on the quality of drugs that you purchase overseas. To prevent any hassle at customs, it is important that your drugs are in the original, labeled containers with your name on them. Drugs that are legal in the US could be illegal elsewhere.

- Travelers' diarrhea is by far the most common travel-related illness. You are at greatest risk when traveling outside northern Europe, Canada, Australia, or the United States. Travelers' diarrhea is most times caused by eating foods contaminated with certain types of bacteria, but it is also caused by the stress or change of diet that come with any international trip.

  Tips for avoiding diarrhea:

  - It's a cliche, but when in suspect countries, don't drink the water. Don't eat the ice cubes. Don't even brush your teeth with it. Don't rinse your mouth out in the shower with it. Drink, brush, and/or rinse with only bottled, boiled, or treated water. Be sure that bottled water is opened in your presence.

  - Avoid unpasteurized dairy products like milk, cream cheese, or pastries with cream or custard filling. Stay away from salad greens or raw fruit and vegetables.

- Business travelers could be at greater risk of contracting AIDS and other diseases than the general population. Why? Because they travel to foreign countries where medical practices and sanitary conditions could be substandard and possibly dangerous. Because of the loneliness of the road, casual sexual encounters and temptations to stray from monogamous relationships are more numerous.

The following are some suggestions for decreasing the risk of contracting AIDS (and other diseases) while on the road:

– Try to avoid sexual contact with casual acquaintances, and avoid prostitutes—in some areas 90 percent are reportedly HIV positive. If engaging in any sexual activity, men must wear condoms at all times.

– Condoms purchased overseas aren't as reliable as those in the US. Heat, light, and time will eventually render latex condoms useless. Always have a fresh supply on hand. As Dr. Erwin Haas says in his *Traveler's Health Guide*: "Protect your condoms and they will protect you."

– Avoid any skin puncturing activity like ear piercing, tattooing, acupuncture, manicures, or dental work—especially when traveling in less-developed countries.

– Consider medical evacuation insurance if you will be traveling to underdeveloped countries. Ask your travel agent how to purchase this.

– Keep up to date on all vaccinations (like tetanus) to avoid injections in foreign countries. If you must have a shot or other medical treatment, contact the local US embassy or consulate for recommendations.

- The traditional "booze, broads, and bribes" culture of business travel has all but disappeared in the United States. But overseas—particularly in parts of the Orient—the tradition persists. And these days, that tradition could prove lethal. Don't risk your life for a deal.

- For long-term assignments, some countries require proof that you are HIV negative before granting you a work visa. For a complete list of international AIDS testing requirements, contact the Bureau of Consular Affairs, 2201 C St. NW, Room 5807, Washington DC, 20520, or call 202-647-1488.

• Hepatitis B (an epidemic of similar proportions) is much more easily transmitted than HIV. Business travelers headed to third world countries for prolonged periods should consider a hepatitis vaccine, unless they are already immune. Many people don't know it, but they are already immune. The vaccine, a series of three shots over six months, costs about $100 and is covered by most health insurance plans.

(Sources: *Corporate Travel Magazine*, various infectious disease specialists.)

| 161 | **Know Conditions Ahead** |

Check the weather ahead by tuning in to the Weather Channel, which gives worldwide forecasts. You can also check *USA TODAY*, or call 1-900-WEATHER. Remember that the seasons are reversed in southern hemisphere cities like Buenos Aires or Sydney, and that rainy or dry seasons are the rule in many equatorial cities. Pack accordingly.

---

162 | Choose the Proper Financial Instruments

The abundance of cheap international airfares is helping to keep the cost of going overseas at an all-time low. But with the US dollar fluctuating, the cost of staying overseas can become a burden that many business travelers can't afford. A good way to start saving money up front is to analyze the changing financial instruments available for international travelers and choose the ones that suit you best. Some considerations:

- Automated Teller Machines (ATMs) are currently your best deal because they dispense local currency—drawing on your home bank account—and give you the wholesale exchange rate, a preferential rate usually reserved for transactions of $1 million or more. This rate can be from 5 percent to 10 percent better than the rate you get at hotels or currency exchanges. Expect similar or slightly higher per-transaction fees than you are charged for ATM withdrawals at home. Tip: Be sure to deposit enough money in your checking account before you leave. The Cirrus and Plus Networks are not combined outside the United States. To find out where you can use your Cirrus card, call 1-800-424-7787. For the Plus System, call your bank. International ATMs accept only four digit PIN code numbers.

- US dollar traveler's checks are losing popularity because of bad exchange rates and usurious bank fees. You'll avoid potentially long waits in line, high fees, and bad conversion rates (especially in the United Kingdom) by buying your traveler's checks here in the currency of the country to which you are headed.

- Always try to purchase enough local currency in the US to pay your cab fare from your destination airport to your hotel, plus a little extra for tips. This way you can avoid the lines that inevitably form at airport currency exchanges. At the airport, it is usually only possible to get the official rate (plus official surcharges) that vary greatly from what you can get on the street. Foreign exchange Ruesch International sells a variety of international currencies over the phone and will send your currency via overnight mail. Call 800-424-2923. Compare their exchange rate with that of your local bank.

- Spend or convert your foreign coins into bills before returning to the United States. Banks and foreign exchanges accept foreign bills only.

- Cash advances on credit cards are a good idea only if you pay off your balance every month. Using your Visa or MasterCard, plus your personal identification number, or PIN, you can withdraw cash from more banks in more countries than you can with only an ATM card.

American Express provides another ATM network. For locations, call 1-800 CASH-NOW. They charge a 2 percent fee on these transactions. However, card holders can avoid the 2 percent by cashing personal checks (for local currency) at American Express offices in most major cities around the world.

- If you pay with a credit card, you avoid fees altogether and get a potentially better exchange rate. If the dollar strengthens between the time you make your purchase and the time it is processed, you'll come out ahead (or vice versa). Most establishments frequented by business travelers around the world accept all major credit cards.

---

163 | Know Your Hotel

- US travelers are spoiled by low rates due to our overbuilt market. Hotel rates for business class accommodations overseas are typically three or four times what you would expect to pay for a similar hotel in the United States.

- Before leaving, ask your travel agent to determine if your hotel has an early check-in policy for international arrivals. Most flights from the East Coast to Europe arrive very early in the morning. Flights from the West Coast to Asia arrive early in the morning as well. There is nothing worse than the jet-lagged, sleep-starved purgatory of sitting in a crowded hotel lobby waiting for maids to clean your room.

- Use the concierge at international hotels. You won't find a better source of local information or assistance.

(For tips using the phone overseas, see Chapter 9.)

---

164 | Understand International Driving

- US state-issued driver's licenses are valid in many countries. If you aren't sure, call the American Automobile Association (AAA). They will issue you an international driving permit for $10. Inquire about the type of car you will be renting—many foreign locations rent only cars with manual transmissions. Check with your insurance company or credit card company before you go to determine coverages.

- If you have several meetings at various locations in a foreign city, ask the hotel concierge to arrange a driver for you for the day, a common practice in many foreign cities. Renting a car and trying to navigate a foreign city could be a lesson in futility.

---

165 | Educate Yourself

- Before leaving the United States, go to your public library and brush up on the politics, economy, geography, and language of the country you will be visiting. The ugly American, although a dying breed, is still the brunt of many jokes in international circles due to a supposed insularity and ignorance of the world beyond our borders.

- Be inquisitive about your host culture. It will flatter your hosts. You'll be surprised to see the eyes of a host countryman light up when you can say a few words in his language, can correctly pronounce his president's or prime minister's name, or can knowledgeably discuss the geography of his homeland.

---

166 Overcome Language Barriers

- Since the majority of Americans are not multilingual, the use of an interpreter is usually necessary. To avoid confusing or offending your foreign counterpart:

  - Don't try to make jokes that are regional, slangy, or sarcastic.

  - Maintain eye contact with your counterpart, not the interpreter.

  - Don't say things you wouldn't want your counterpart to hear. Many foreigners can understand English, but lack the confidence to speak it.

  - Speak slowly and keep negotiations as concise as possible.

  (Source: *The Executive Speaker*, Orlando, Florida)

---

167 Understand International Protocol

- The smart international traveler will do some cultural research to prevent committing embarrassing gaffes abroad. Business travelers need to be especially alert for behavior that could not only offend a host, but could doom a deal. Your local bookstore travel section is full of helpful how-to guides for travel abroad, but most are written with the vacation traveler in mind. To find the ones of assistance to the business traveler requires a little digging.

- Offering extensive details about foreign customs, courtesies, and cultural differences are the European and Asia Pacific Travel organizers from Austin House (1-800-268-5157), a large supplier of travel-related information and accessories. The best part about these guides is that they come in loose-leaf binders, so you don't have to haul around all the details of doing business in Singapore, Hong Kong, or Taiwan when you are only going to be in Bangkok. The guide allows you to select only the countries relevant to your itinerary and leave the rest behind.

- An excellent source of country specific information are *Culturgrams*, published by the David M. Kennedy Center for International Studies at Brigham Young University in Provo, Utah. The short four-page briefings have the unique ability to go beyond the superficial demographics and reveal a nation's personality, lifestyle, and culture. Each individual briefing paper is written by a native of the selected nation, or someone who has lived there for at least three years and is fluent in one of its major languages. Every *Culturgram* is revised and updated yearly. Order *Culturgrams* individually ($4.99), by the set (prices vary), or by calling 800-528-6279.

168 | Women Take Note

Outside the US and some northern European countries, women traveling on business do not usually receive the same amount of respect as their male counterparts. Although female business travelers account for one of the fastest growing segments of the travel industry, the problem persists. "One possible advantage to businesswomen encountering a foreign society is that their associates may be a bit curious and more apt to pay attention—and test their competence," says Terrell Mellen, an international business traveler and marketing manager for the Washington DC- based Air Travel Card.

An informal poll of female business travelers conducted by the Air Travel Card provides these tips:

- Research the customs of the country you are visiting before boarding the plane. Familiarity with local and regional attitudes about women in business will help define your approach and avoid potential problems or embarrassing situations.

- When you arrive, observe local businesswomen and adapt your practices accordingly. Do not lose your identity, but be sensitive to the woman's role.

- In some countries it may be helpful (or the law) to travel with a male escort who can serve as a buffer between the two societies. In some instances, having a man introduce you can immediately establish credibility in a business situation.

- Carry plenty of business cards with your business information printed on the reverse in the official language of your host country. Your business card makes a professional impression, establishes credibility, and assists in introductions when conversing in a foreign language.

- Maintain your sense of humor! Often, problems on the road are a result of cultural differences and not sex discrimination. Try to defuse these incidents by keeping them in the proper context, then add them to your repertoire of international travel anecdotes.

---

169 | Play It Safe Abroad (Bonus Tips)

- DON'T BRING SENSITIVE THINGS TO SENSITIVE AREAS
  For example, don't try to bring a bottle of booze or a *Playboy* magazine or your copy of *Satanic Verses* to an Islamic country. This awareness is part of learning about the country before you go.

- BEWARE OF PEOPLE CAUSING DISTRACTIONS
  Scams used by pickpockets, thieves, and assorted n'er-do- wells: An offer to brush lint off your suit; accidently spilling or spewing catsup, mustard, or other condiment on your clothing; a little old lady drops her suitcase and you help her. Before you know it, you've been had. Also, crafty pickpockets will stand next to the signs that say "Beware of Pickpockets" just to watch where people feel to see if their wallet is still there. Then they know exactly where to "pick."

- DURING TIME OF HEIGHTENED INTERNATIONAL TENSION:

  - Avoid Public Areas
    Likely targets of terrorist activities—bus/train/subway stations, government plazas. Many times disturbances will happen around public or religious holidays and controversial anniversary dates.

  - Keep a Low Profile
    Americans have a reputation for standing out. Try to blend in.

OUT OF TOWN SHOULD NEVER MEAN OUT OF TOUCH.

With the flights, hotels and rentals, any business trip can become exhausting and make your family and home feel even farther away. But you are on the road for a reason and good business requires good communication. The same is true for families. Which is why it makes sense to carry the MCI Preferred Card.^{SM} Because now when you apply, MCI will give you **one month of free calls.*** It's also one easy way to keep a business trip from turning into a guilt trip.

1-800-727-6241

TO GET ONE MONTH OF FREE CALLS:

Receive your FREE MCI PREFERRED CARD^{SM} and **one month of free calls*** for your business travel by completing and mailing back this pre-addressed postcard or calling **1-800-727-6241.**

COMPANY NAME: _____

CONTACT NAME: _____

STREET ADDRESS: _____

CITY: _____ STATE: _____ ZIP: _____

BUSINESS TELEPHONE: _____

NAME TO BE PRINTED ON CARD: _____ # OF CARDS _____

SIGNATURE _____

☐ Check here if you would like information on PROOF POSITIVE^{SM} from MCI or to order cards for other employees in your company.

FOR A MONTH OF FREE CALLS SEE REVERSE SIDE.

12

Tips 170–187
Eating Right

Eating well can be one of the great joys of an otherwise monotonous trip, so always make an effort to get out and enjoy a good meal. It may be the closest thing to a "cultural experience" you'll have on your trips to the less exciting business travel destinations on your itinerary. America has become a world-class diner's market. Indeed, the case can be made that the United States now holds the title to the "Dining Capital of the World" not only in quality, but also in value and sheer variety of international and regional cuisines.

The reasons for this welcome development merit examination by business travelers who are among the many unsung, but well-fed top restaurant critics. Some of the factors that continue to drive America's culinary eminence are:

- *Widespread travel across the United States—by overseas visitors as well as American business and leisure travelers—focuses on regional homegrown foods and styles of eating.*

- *Broad availability of fresh produce, fruit, meat, and other ingredients have elevated cooking at a local level.*

- *Superstar status of American chefs and acceptance of cooking arts as a valid career path of young people.*

- *Several decades of demographic and lifestyle changes that have drawn more meals outside the home and created a generation that has grown up accustomed to eating in restaurants.*

- *New waves of immigrant cultures bringing diverse and inexpensive strains of ethnic cooking—from Asia, South America, the Caribbean, and Africa.*

170 Find the Right Meal

- Perhaps the most up-to-date and authoritative voices in American cuisine belong to Tina and Tim Zagat, publishers of the well-known *Zagat Surveys*. For the business traveler, the Zagats recently published their first two national dining guides: *America's Top Restaurants* and *America's Best Value Restaurants*. With input from nearly 30,000 frequent diners across the country, the two pocket-sized, easily packed books chart a unique, consumerwise portrait of America's food scene in 29 US cities (call Zagat at 1-800-333-3421).

- If you are on a long-term assignment in one city or travel to one city frequently, you may opt for the more detailed individual *Zagat Surveys* covering 21 metropolitan areas in the US. The *Zagat Surveys* are available in most major bookstores for $9.95. The national editions cost $12.95.

- Can't decide between bagels, Burmese, Thai, or Tandoori and not staying in a New York hotel with a good concierge? Just call (212) 777-FOOD, and you can access an instant review of over 3,000 New York area restaurants on a new free service called Foodphone. In addition to basic food type, location, and price range information, Foodphone highlights restaurants famous for brunches, desserts, views, romance, "hot new openings," and New Yorkers' favorite restaurants for each food type. Foodphone has secured "XXX-FOOD" numbers in nine other metropolitan markets and will begin offering the service in these cities in 1994.

- A savvy cabbie or good hotel concierge is always a good source.

GENERAL TIPS

Harried business travelers who juggle meetings with flight schedules and leave little time for healthy eating may find that all their haste may be making more "waist."

---

171 Don't skip breakfast. A healthy breakfast helps boost your energy and control your appetite through the day. Eat a balanced meal such as muffins, cereal with milk, and juice.

---

172 Avoid those cheap but deadly breakfast buffets heaped high with fried eggs, bacon, and hash browns. A breakfast like that will more likely slow you down than pick you up. A few chunks of pale, unripe cantaloupe is typically the healthiest offering you'll find on one of these groaning boards.

---

173 Be choosy about restaurants. If you are not out to impress a client, family style restaurants or cafeterias usually offer nutritional items like salads, steamed vegetables, and baked or grilled meats. A good, inexpensive, and interesting vegetarian restaurant can usually be found near a college campus.

---

174 Check menus before you sit down. Steer clear of fatty foods like red meat, cream sauces, fried foods, and heavy desserts. Airport restaurants, fast food establishments, and fern bars serve primarily high-fat, high-cholesterol fare.

175 When you are picking up the tab, take the lead when ordering. If you decide to get the healthy choice, it's likely that everyone else at the table may tone down their appetite.

176 Don't fall into the unhealthy trap of thinking you should order "the biggest" or "the most expensive" at restaurants simply because you're on an expense account or someone else is picking up the tab. Also, remember that you do not have to "clean your plate."

177 Pack some raisins, dried apricots, an apple, orange, or a bagel in your brief case or carry-on bag. This way you'll be less tempted by the high-fat, high-salt, high-preservative fare from airplane galleys or vending machines.

178 Drink less. Business travelers tend to drink more on the road than at home. Alcohol is high in calories, magnifies the effects of jet lag, and generally slows you down. Try to drink more water and natural fruit juices instead, which will help energize you and keep you at peak performance levels.

179 Avoid hotel minibars, usually crammed full of high-priced, high-sodium, artificially preserved snacks. Instead, visit a nearby market and buy some fresh fruit to snack on during your stay. If you do break down and drink one of those $3 cans of soda pop or $2 candy bars, replace it with the same store-bought item to save money.

180   A growing number of hotels now stock minibars with helpful, inexpensive necessities, like mineral water, crackers and cheese, milk and cookies, pretzels and fruit juice—all at less than premium prices.

181   And now, even nonfood items are making their way into the minibar—almost transforming them into personal in-room convenience stores. Depending on the hotel, you can now find disposable cameras, disposable razors, suntan lotion, Band-Aids, "hangover kits," and playing cards. One progressive minibar offering: condoms.

182   For longer stays, choose a hotel that offers kitchen facilities. With the option of preparing your own meals, you have more control over what you eat.

183   Order your airline meals in advance. Most major carriers offer special low-fat, low-cholesterol, or other special meals. (See Chapter 6.) Like the airlines, many hotel banquet facilities now accommodate requests for vegetarian, low-sodium, low-fat, or other meals. Inquire with the hotel

banquet staff or meeting planner in charge of the meal.

---

184 Choose restaurants with healthful alternatives to rich foods and sauces. Ethnic foods like Chinese, Thai, and Italian can offer good taste with relatively little saturated fat and cholesterol.

---

185 As the US travel industry prepares for an influx of foreign business travelers, hoteliers and airlines are now expanding their offerings to help satisfy the cravings of their international guests. International food offerings provide an interesting option for travelers who want to make an otherwise mundane business trip into a bit of an adventure.

- Westin Hotels & Resorts now serve an authentic Japanese breakfast featuring pick-led vegetables, rice, fish sausage, and roasted seaweed.

- Bunderfliesch or thin slices of air-dried beef, and Birchermuesli, a mixture of yogurt, nuts, grains, and dried fruit popular with Europeans, are available at Swissôtels in the US.

- Northwest and Delta provide Japan-bound business-class passengers with makanouchi, a chilled meal consisting of shrimp or sliced beef, rice, pickled vegetables, and miso soup served in a black-lacquered box. They are also available to passengers taking only the domestic leg (i.e., New York to Los Angeles) of these international flights.

| 186 | **Eating Out Alone Is OK** |

One of the banes of the business travel experience is the trauma of having to eat out alone. Have you ever returned to your hotel after a long day's work and thought you would skip room service and just step down the street for a bite at that corner bistro, but could not bear the thought of sitting alone? It doesn't have to be that way. Here are some solutions:

- Find friends. Sit at sushi bars or Captain's tables to find other lonely souls looking for dinner mates.

- Bring something to do. A book, magazine, or some other light reading can ease your feelings of awkwardness or loneliness.

- Avoid high-priced, exclusive restaurants if you can. A fast and friendly place like TGI Friday's, Bennigan's, or similar establishments aren't so bad, especially if you sit at a table in the bar area. A TV in the bar usually helps. You get your food fast and can get out fast.

- Eating alone in a hotel restaurant isn't as severe because it is more likely that several other people will be eating alone too. Staff at hotel restaurants are more accustomed to "a table for one." If your hotel doesn't have a restaurant, head to a nearby hotel with one.

- Get used to it. Veteran business travelers claim that after a while, they cross a threshold, and eating out alone doesn't really bother them anymore.

- Call your friends, or friends of your friends. Invite them to go out with you.

- Room service. If all else fails, try room service. Remember you don't always have to go by the measly room service menu usually offered—you can ask for almost anything you want.

- Cook in your room. With average guest stays of around 14 days, extended stay hotels with kitchens or kitchenettes allow business travelers the luxury of an almost home cooked meal.

| 187 |

For those who choose to eat fast food around the world, here's what they can expect to pay for a cheeseburger, soft drink, and french fries in 12 different cities:

Barcelona, Spain	$3.45
Berlin, Germany	$5.94
Buenos Aires, Argentina	$7.00
Cairo, Egypt	$2.17
Copenhagen, Denmark	$8.34
Hong Kong	$2.69
London, England	$5.35
Los Angeles, US	$3.77
Mexico City, Mexico	$5.24
Sydney, Australia	$5.19
Tel Aviv, Israel	$4.82
Tokyo, Japan	$6.82

(Prices in January 1994. Source: *Runzheimer International*.)

Tips 188–202
Staying Healthy and
Managing Stress

"Lift that carry-on and run to the gate,
Then sit for hours because the plane is late!
Struggle up the aisle and drop into your seat,
With stinging eyes and swollen feet.
By the time you get home, your body feels like
concrete!"

Alice Stevens

The best way to reduce travel-related stress is to stay in peak condition. "Frequent travelers should shape up for the rigors of the road like athletes train for the rigors of competition," says corporate fitness instructor Alice Stevens. Indeed, a strong, healthy body can handle stress better than a weak one. Some tips for staying fit:

---

188 | Stay Fit in Flight

- Be aware of how you sit on the plane or in your car. Good posture is essential when battling the stress associated with sitting in cramped quarters for hours. On long flights, try some in-seat movements (shoulder/head rolls, knee lifts, systematic tensing and relaxing of different muscle groups) and move around the airplane cabin as much as possible.

- To prevent dehydration, drink one eight ounce glass of water or juice for every hour you are in flight. Alcohol, caffeine, and some nasal decongestants can magnify dehydration. Contact lens wearers should carry extra saline solution.

- In flight, breathe through your nose instead of your mouth. Your nose is the body's first and best defense against concentrations of airborne germs in the recirculated cabin air.

- For back support, place a small pillow in the seat just above your pelvis. To prevent pressure on the sciatic nerve, men should move their wallets from back pocket to their front or breast pocket. Suffer from swollen feet and ankles? Both men and women should consider wearing elastic or support hose on long flights.

- When you land, find a quiet smoke-free space for some deep breathing exercises. This should help get your blood gases back to normal and reduce stress.

(See Chapter 6 for more in-flight tips.)

---

189 | Maintain Your Exercise Regimen

- Remember, traveling itself takes a toll on your body. Don't work out any harder on the road than you do at home. Always remember to warm up and cool down slowly.

- Ask if your hotel has an exercise room, gym, or fitness center. Does your health club at home have reciprocal agreements with others around the country? If you are in the habit of exercising at home, try to fit in some type of exercise when you are on the road—even if it is only a few stretches on the hotel room floor.

- At more luxurious hotels, you can request fitness equipment in your room. Manhattan's Lowell Hotel offers the ultimate in-room workout opportunity, the "Gym Suite." The one-bedroom suite has a separate room with a Stairmaster, treadmill, stationary bicycle, free weights, ballet bar, and Nautilus system, and mirrored walls. Six Hilton Suites' properties offer in-room exercise equipment for an extra $7 to $15 per night. Hotel valets at the Pan Pacific Hotel in San Francisco deliver Stairmasters, rowing machines, treadmills, or free weights to guest rooms, and more important, remove them as soon as the guest is finished.

- Other less luxurious in-room options to bring from home: jumpropes, aerobic dance or yoga tapes. An in-room exercise manual at Residence Inns (called *Inn Shape*) exhorts "phone book leg lifts, lower abdominal bed crunches, and shoulder and tricep towel extensions," as part of the Heart Association's recommendation of 30 to 60 minutes of exercise three to four times a week. (For the free guide, call Residence Inn at 301-380-4536).

- For a psychological boost, make exercise a goal of your trip. On some long travel days, the only goal you may attain will be completing your exercise routine. If you are able to get a workout at the end of a long day you'll feel like you are living up to at least one of your goals.

- Indulge yourself with a massage, whirlpool, or sauna, if your hotel offers it. These can reduce the physical tension of sitting for long periods in stuffy planes and airports.

- Walk whenever possible: upstairs, shopping, or to a meeting. The exercise you get will make a difference in how you feel.

OTHER HEALTH TIPS

What with cramped and stuffy airplane cabins, airport gates full of unrepentant smokers, diesel fumes, and dirty hotel rooms, staying healthy on the road can be a difficult task.

---

190 Look for hotels that offer environmentally sound or "green rooms," which usually feature recycling programs for their paper, glass, and cardboard, and so forth. The Marriott-Dadeland in Miami kicked off this trend in 1992, and other hotel chains and individual hotels are slowly joining in. Their green rooms are usually cleaned and treated to remove any residual odors. They install equipment that purifies the room's air and drinking water. Filters installed in bathrooms remove the chlorine and any bad taste or odor from the local water. Also featured: low-flow showerheads and toilets, all natural shampoos and soaps, and natural fiber carpeting. Ask your travel agent or hotel reservationist about the availability of green rooms.

---

191 If you have grown accustomed to smoke-free flying on domestic routes, you may be startled to board international flights and find cigarette smoke once again curling from behind your seatback. However, Air Canada, Cathay Pacific, and British Airways on some US-based carriers are experimenting with nonsmoking international flights. Always ask about this possibility.

STRESS MANAGEMENT

192 | Manage Your Stress

Stress, that feeling of being overwhelmed by the responsibilities and problems of everyday life, can have a serious negative impact on mental and physical health, not to mention productivity. Much research has been done on how life on the road affects frequent travelers and their families.

First, here are some general issues to concentrate on when battling the stress of a life on the road.

1. *Diet*. Don't go overboard when traveling. Take advantage of the new lighter fare menus. Avoid the depressive effect of alcohol.

2. *Exercise routine*. Try to stick to your at-home routine when on the road.

3. *Meditation/journaling*. Make time to sit quietly and reflect on the day, or keep a daily journal of your thoughts and feelings.

4. *Support group*. Find other frequent travelers to share your feelings with. Remember, you are not alone in your frustration.

5. *Environmental control.* Bring along a picture of your spouse and put it on your bedside table, or bring along a small pillow. Try to impose your own environment onto the ever changing on-the-road environment. Manage your environment instead of letting it manage you.

---

193 Don't try to cram all your travel into one day. Sometimes it's worth the hotel expense to arrive the night before and get a good night's sleep.

---

194 Don't feel bad about making "too many long-distance calls." Set up an answering machine at home and check your messages regularly. Return calls from afar. The telephone is your connection to your personal life, which needs to be nurtured, not ignored, even when you are away.

---

195 In the current environment, it's inevitable that you will encounter delays. Always come prepared with pleasant distractions like a book, a magazine, a new tape or CD for your Walkman, or a project that you are working on.

---

196 Don't feel guilty about taking a break. Attend a local sporting event, see a movie, visit old friends, see museums or libraries, walk through interesting neighborhoods or markets. Try to restore a sense of adventure to your trip.

---

197 Consider joining an airline airport club. They are ideal places to relax, accomplish work, or make calls. They are also a good place to find a support group of other frequent travelers. Even if your company won't pay for this luxury, it may be worth paying for yourself ($100–$200 per year; Continental offers a $30 one-month trial membership).

FOR YOUR FAMILY

After a grueling week on the road, a business traveler looks forward to rest and relaxation at home. But the stay-at-home spouse, eager to make up for lost time, expects a lot of quality time from the traveling spouse. These differing expectations can wreak havoc on what should be "loving" homecomings.

A University of South Carolina study headed by psychology professor Frederick Medway determined what stay-at-home spouses want from their traveling spouses on their return:

- 71 percent want to be told they are missed.
- 30 percent want the traveling spouse to spend time parenting the children.
- 25 percent want affection and sex.

On the other hand, of returning travelers:
- 29 percent prefer rest.
- 24 percent want a clean house.
- 14 percent want a home-cooked meal.

| 198 | Based on their 1994 survey of business travelers, MCI offers these tips for staying close: videotape special occasions, send postcards, have set times to call home, bring home gifts, save memorabilia,

bring along pictures or children's drawings, and send flowers. Another good idea: hide notes or gifts at home and call in your instructions on how to find them.

199 | Bring along a companion every now and then, if possible. Many conventions and hotels now provide child care. It's psychologically beneficial for family members to see what you do while traveling. It can ease their feelings of resentment, and your feelings of guilt.

200 | Many new-fangled phone cards (and even some pay phones) allow callers to program a message to be delivered at any time. If you will be on an extended trip or otherwise out of touch, leave a short "I love/miss/can't-wait-to-see/am-thinking-of you" message for each day that you are away.

201 | The 1989 Hyatt Travel Futures Project survey of 700 business travelers found that some are less prone to stress than others. "Road warriors" or model travelers are flexible, easy-going, and actually enjoy a certain amount of pressure. The survey found that many business travelers take their business trips too seriously. They tend to make the trips the focus of their lives, instead of accepting business travel as part of their normal routine. Well-adjusted travelers are those who have learned to anticipate and handle uncertainties, have a good sense of humor, and are realistic about the business world and its limitations.

| 202 | According to research by Residence Inns, women traveling on business enjoy leaving the responsibilities of keeping house at home. While on the road they are able to focus on themselves or on their work without domestic distractions. "The in-room experience can be more nourishing to a woman than a man," said project consultant Dr. Ron Jones. |

(Sources: The Marriott Business Travel Institute, the Hyatt Travel Futures Project, psychologists Deborah Butler and Frederick Medway, MCI/Gallup Survey of Business Travelers.)

APPENDIX

Telephone Resources

CHAPTER 2

For Subscription Information:
USA *Today* 1-800-USA-0001
The Wall Street Journal 1-800-228-6262
New York Times 1-800-631-2580
Travel and Leisure 1-800-888-8728
Condé Nast Traveler 1-800-777-0700
InsideFlyer 1-800-333-5937
Frequent Flyer 1-800 323 3537
Best Fares 1-800-635-3033
Business Travel News/Corporate Travel
  1-800-964-9494

CHAPTER 4

Car Services:
  Tel Aviv 1-212-777-777
  Jerusalem 1-212-996-6600
  Sabra 1-212-777-7171

NY/NJ Port Authority Ground Transportation
  1-800-AIR-RIDE

Salk International's *Airport Transit Guide*:
  1-714-893-0812

CHAPTER 5

Offical Airline Guide 1-800-323-3537

Complaints:
US Department of Transportation
1-202-366-2220

CHAPTER 6

Federal Aviation Administration 1-800-FAA-SURE

Pegasus Fear of Flying Foundation
1-800-FEAR-NOT

American Airlines Fearless Flyers 1-800-451-5106

Freedom from Fear of Flying 1-305-261-7042

CHAPTER 8

Discount Hotel Reservations:
Hotel Reservations Network 1-800-964-6835
QuikBook 1-800-221-3531

CHAPTER 9

Long Distance Network Access Lines:
AT&T 1-800-321-0ATT
MCI 1-800-950-1022
Sprint 1-800-877-8000

CHAPTER 10

Frequent Flyer Services 1-719-597-8889

Frequent Flyer Guidebook 1-800-333-5937

CHAPTER **11**

US State Department:
Passport Information 1-202-647-0518
Consular Affairs Bulletin Board (modem)
1-800 647-9225
Travel Advisories 1-202-647-5225

American Express Emergency Assist:
1-202-783-7474

Immunizations/Vaccinations:
Centers for Disease Control 1-404-639-2572
AIDS Testing Requirements 1-202-647-1488

International Weather 1-900-WEATHER
($.95 per minute)

ATMs:
Cirrus Network Locations 1-800-424-7787
American Express 1-800-CASH-NOW

Currency Exchange-Ruesch International
1-800-424-2923

Asia-Pacific/European Travel Guides
1-800-268-5157

Brigham Young Univ. *CulturGrams*
1-800-528-6279

CHAPTER **12**

Zagat Surveys 1-800-333-3421
FoodPhone (New York City) 1-212-777-FOOD

CHAPTER **13**

Residence Inn *InnShape Guide* 1-301-380-4536

About the Author

As director of Atlanta-based Travel Skills Group, author Christopher McGinnis consults, writes, and leads seminars on and about business travel. It is his company's premise that **educated** travelers are happier, more productive, and more efficient executives in the field.

Upon earning a Master's degree in international business in 1984, McGinnis was hired as a management consultant for an international firm and spent the next four years as a business traveler across the US and around the world. Based on this experience and the need he saw for better-informed business travelers, McGinnis launched Travel Skills Group in 1988. Since then, he has addressed thousands of travelers at major corporate meetings and training programs nationwide.

McGinnis writes a weekly column for business travelers in the Atlanta *Journal-Constitution*, and a monthly column for business owners in *Entrepreneur* magazine.

INDEX

A

Accounting code, 86
AIDS, 107-9
Airfares, 11-12
  and ticketing, 12-13
Air France coach system, 34
Airline deregulation, 38
Airline entertainment systems,
  58-59
Airline meals, 16, 54-56, 125
Airline reservations, 11-12
Airlines
  complaints to, 44
  on-time performance, 14-15,
  40-41
Airline ticketing, 12-13
Airplanes
  propeller-driven versus jets, 62
  safety tips, 60-62
  seating, 52
Airport clubs, 44-45
Airport codes, 47
Airports
  buses and vans, 31
  car services, 30
  hotel shuttle, 32
  meeting family members, 31
  precautions at, 46-49
  rail connections, 30-31
  taxis, 29-30
  transfer services, 32-35
  travelers' rights, 38
  traveling to, 28-29
Airport Transit Guide, 32

Airport waitlist, 45
Air Travel Card, 116
America's Best Value Restaurants,
  121
America's Top Restaurants, 121
American Airlines fearless flying
  classes, 60
American Association of Retired
  Persons, 73
American Automobile
  Association, 67, 73, 113
American Express, 106
American Society of Travel
  Agents, 15
Association discounts, 73
Austin House, 115
Auto insurance, 67-68
Automated teller machines,
  110-12

B

Back-to-back fare, 12
Bed-and-breakfast
  establishments, 79
Best Fares, 9
Boarding pass, 45
Bomb scenes, 48-49
Booze-broads-and-bribes culture,
  109
Boston Airport Water Shuttle, 33
Boutique hotels, 79
Breakfast, 122
British Airways, 53

143

Bromley, Stan, 76
Bulkhead seats, 52
Bumping policy, 41-43
Bureau of Consular Affairs, 109
Business-class hotel rooms, 72-74
Business class sections, 53
Business travel magazines, 9
Business Travel News, 9
Business travel survey, 4

C

Car jacking, 69-70
Car phones, 66
Car rental
  counter, 64-66
  driving tips, 66-67
  international, 113
  international driving, 67
  reservations, 13-14
  safety tips, 68-70
Car services, 30
Cash advances, 111-12
CD players, 59
Centers for Disease Control, 106
Chicago-O'Hare Airport, 33
Cirus network, 110
Citizen's Emergency Center, 105
Citizenship, proof of, 103-4
Clothing, selection of, 21-22
Collision damage waiver, 67
Complaints
  to airlines, 44
  to hotels, 76
Computerized low fare/seat
  finder, 10
Consortium rate, 74
Consular Affairs Bulletin Board,
  105
Consumer affairs offices, 44
Continental Airlines, 53

Contract of carriage, 38
  bumping policy, 41
  rule 240, 39
Corporate rates, 72-73
Corporate Travel Magazine, 109
Courtesy phones, 33
Credit calling cards, 85-86
Credit calling card thieves, 47-48,
  89
Credit card cash advances, 111-
  12
Credit card companies, auto
  insurance, 67-68
Culturgrams, 115
Currency, 111

D

David M. Kennedy Center for
  International Studies, 115
Debit cards, 86-87
Department of Transportation,
  44
Diarrhea, 107
Dining alone, 126-27
Do-not-disturb signs, 80
Drinking, 123
Driver's license, 113
Driving safety, 68-70
Driving tips, 66-67
Drugs, legal and illegal, 107
Dusseldorf, Germany, 35

E

Ear problems, 57-58
Eating, 120-27
Economy hotels, 78
Ehret, Charles, 57
Elite level programs, 94-95

Elite level upgrades, 95-96
Emergency assistance numbers,
    106
Excess valuation insurance, 44
Exercise regimen, 131-33
Extended-stay hotels, 78-79

F

Family
    keeping in touch with, 136-38
    meeting at airports, 31
Fast food prices, 127
Fear of flying, 59-60
Federal Communications
    Commission, 85
Financial instruments, 110-12
Fire escape/survival procedures,
    79-80
First class, 46, 53
Flight cancellations, 40
Flight delays, 39-40
Foodphone, 121
Foreign exchange, 111
Frankfurt, Germany, 34-35
Freedom from Fear of Flying,
    Inc., 60
Frequent Flyer Magazine, 9, 97
Frequent Flyer Services, 99-100
Frequent renter programs, 66
Frequent traveler programs
    elite levels, 94-95
    expiration of miles, 98
    information sources, 99-100
    number of, 16
    partner programs, 98-99
    planning ahead, 96-97
    selecting, 92-94
    updating information, 97-98
    upgrading tickets, 95-96

G

Gallup Organization, 57
Gate-checked bags, 24
Geneva, Switzerland, 34

H

Haas, Erwin, 108
Headphones, 54
Health
    tips on, 133-34
    while flying, 130-31
Hepatitis B, 109
Hidden-city fare, 12-13
Hilton Hotels, phone policy, 84
Hindu meals, 55
Hitchhikers, 70
HIV virus, 108-9
Homecomings, 136
Host culture, 114
Hotel industry classifications, 76-
    79
Hotel minibars, 124
Hotel reservations, 13
    direct, 16
Hotel Reservations Network, 74
Hotels
    business-class rooms, 72-74
    complaints to, 76
    and frequent flyer programs,
        99
    frequent stay programs, 98-99
    information about, 121
    in international travel, 112-13
    phone calls from, 75-76, 84-85
    problems at, 74-75
    room rates, 72-74
    safety tips, 79-81
Hotel safes, 80
Hotel shuttle, 32
Hyatt Travel Futures Project, 137

I

Illness, 106-9
Immunizations, 106
In-flight fitness, 130-31
Information
    frequent flyer programs, 97-98, 99-100
    on travel industry, 8-9
InsideFlyer, 9, 97, 99
Internal Revenue Service, 100
International calling, 88-89
International driving, 67-68, 113
International Foundation of Airline Passenger Associations, 61
International protocol, 114-16
International travel, 102-3
    documents for, 103-5
    education about, 113-14
    fast food prices, 127
    financial instruments, 110-12
    health tips, 106-9
    hotels, 112-13
    planning for, 105-6
    weather conditions, 109-10
    women travelers, 116-17

J-K

Jet lag, 56-57
Jones, Ron, 138
KLM, 53
Kosher meals, 54-55

L

La Guardia Airport, 30, 33
Language barriers, 114
Laptop computers, 59
Limo companies, 30

Long-distance calls, 75-76
Lufthansa transfer services, 34-35
Luggage
    carry-on, 23-24
    choosing, 20-21
    lost, 43-44
    unattended, 48
Luggage tags, 21, 46-47
Luggage trollies, 20
Luxury hotels, 77

M

MCI/Gallup survey, 4
Meals, 121-22
Medical evacuation insurance, 108
Melatonin, 57
Milan, Linate Airport, 32
Mileage banks, 100
Mileage saver plans, 97
Modems, 105
Moderate hotels, 78
Moslem meals, 55
Motor clubs, 65
Munich airport, 33

N

Newark Airport, 30
New York City, 30
New York Times travel section, 8
Nonstop flights, 17
No-surcharge calling cards, 86

O

Off-airport car rentals, 65
Official Airline Guide, 39-40

Official Frequent Flyer Guidebook, 100

Off-peak travel time, 97

On-time performance data, 14-15, 40-41

Oregon Health Services University, 57

Overcoming Jet Lag (Ehret), 57

Overseas assignments, 102-3

P

Packing tips, 23

Paris, France, 34

Parking lots
dangers, 46
unguarded, 69

Partner programs, 98-99

Passports, 102-4

Pay phones, 84-85

Pegasus Fear of Flying Foundation, 60

Personal 800 service, 87-88

Petersen, Randy, 99-100

Photocopying documents, 105-6

Pickpockets, 118

Plus network, 110

Preflight announcements, 62

Prescription drugs, 107

Priority seating, 52-53

Propeller-driven airplanes, 62

Protocol, 114-16

Purchased upgrades, 96

Q-R

Quality hotels, 77

Rail connections, 30-31

Rapid rail service, 30-31

Refueling options, 65-66

Residence Inns, 137-38

Restaurants, information sources, 121-22

Road maps, 69

Roadside emergency kit, 69

Roll-aboard suitcases, 20-21

Room deliveries, 80

Ruesch International, 111

Rule 240, 39

S

Safety card, 62

Safety tips
airplanes, 61-62
car rental, 68-70
in hotels, 79-81
seating, 60-61

Salk International Airport Transit Guide, 32

Seat assignment, 16

Seat belts, 61

Seating, 52-54
safety tips, 61

Security checkpoints, 48

Shoulder surfers, 47-48, 89

Shuttle bus service, 31

Sleeper service, 53

Sleep medications, 57

Smoking, 62, 133-34

Southern hemisphere seasons, 110

Spare tires, 68-69

Sporting events, 16

Standard mileage rate deduction, 67

Standby list, 45

State Department, 103, 106
Citizen's Emergency Center, 105

Stevens, Alice, 130

Stevenson, Robert Louis, 52

Stouffer Hotels, phone policy, 84
Stress management, 134-36
Stuttgart, Germany, 35
Suite hotels, 78-79

T

Taxes, standard mileage rate, 67
Taxis, 29-30
Telephone calls, 75-76
    from hotels or pay phones, 84-85
    international, 88-89
Telephone credit card, 85-86
Telephone 800 service, 87-88
Ticketing, 12-13
Toilet kits, 22
Tokyo, Narita Airport, 32
Tone generators, 89
Travel eating tips, 122-26
Travel advisories, 105
Travel agents, 9-10
Travel and Leisure, 8
Traveler, 9
Traveler's Health Guide (Haas), 108
Traveler's checks, 111
Traveler's rights, 38
Travel industry, 8-9
Travel magazines, 8-9
Travel scams, 15
Travel shows, 16
Travel Skills Group, 5
Travels with a Donkey (Stevenson), 52
Travel vouchers, 42
TWA, 53

U-V

Upgrade certificates, 95-96
USA TODAY, 5, 110
    Money section, 8, 97
Vaccinations, 108-9
Van shuttles, 31
Visas, 104-5

W-Z

The Wall Street Journal, 8
Warsaw Convention, 43
Weapons, 48
Weather Channel, 109-10
Westin Hotels and Resorts, 125
Women
    and home responsibilities, 137-38
    in international travel, 116-17
Wright brothers, 92
Wrinkle-free clothing, 21-22
Zagat, Tim, 121
Zagat, Tina, 121
Zagat Surveys, 121